The Ministry of the Saints

Dr. Mark Hanby

with Roger Roth

The Ministry of the Saints

of the

Saints

Rediscovering the Destiny
of Every Believer

Destiny Image® Publishers, Inc.

P.O. Box 310
Shippensburg, PA 17257-0310

*"Speaking to the Purposes of God for This Generation
and for the Generations to Come"*

ISBN 0-7684-2219-1

For Worldwide Distribution

Printed in the U.S.A.

This book and all other Destiny Image, Revival Press, MercyPlace,
Fresh Bread, Destiny Image Fiction, and Treasure House books are available
at Christian bookstores and distributors worldwide.

1 2 3 4 5 6 7 8 9 10 / 10 09 08 07 06 05

For a U.S. bookstore nearest you, call
1-800-722-6774.

For more information on foreign distributors, call
717-532-3040.

Or reach us on the Internet:
www.destinyimage.com

DEDICATION

To the memory of Ernest Doggette a genuine man of God who desired to see the manifestation of ministry through the saints. He understood that the five-fold ministry of apostle, prophet, evangelist, pastor and teacher are largely entrusted with ministry to the saints while biblical ministry to the world would be a ministry of the saints. Ernest, along with his wife Ruth, lovingly compiled information from my audio tapes and provided other materials that have become the foundation of much of this book.

TABLE OF CONTENTS

Author's Note

By simply picking up this book you have entered a high-risk zone!!! By opening these pages you have placed yourself directly in the crosshairs of spiritual alteration. This is where religion is put on trial for its life and tradition begs for mercy. Only the divinely discontented pass through the portals of these pages with any comfort because here, without fear, we will challenge the very existence of our present opinion of ministry.

When I first began teaching Church government and spiritual order more years ago than I wish to recall, I followed the normal established pattern of gathering the "leadership" of the church I was pastoring. This handful of elders, deacons and teachers became the recipient of "confidential" information, which we concluded was far too deep for the average church member to comprehend. I later realized that in order for the **saints** to fulfill their purpose in the Kingdom this "classified" teaching needed to become the foundation of every member, not just of a chosen few.

Now after all these years I am still summoned by pastors to teach leadership on Friday evenings and Saturday mornings and then preach a "normal" sermon on Sunday morning to the general congregation. We still do not understand that we (the accepted ministry) minister to the **saints** so that the saints may, with maturity and understanding, minister to their world. *Set Ministry, Multiplicity of Ministry, Spiritual Authority* and *Membership Maturity* should be Christian education 101.

In this book, *The Ministry of the Saints,* I am doing what may be called "letting the cat out of the bag." I am certain that the advocates of centralization of pulpit power and the proponents of franchised forms of leadership will scream "bloody murder," but this is not the first time that I have squared off with musty tradition and moldy religious ideology. We must bravely examine our deficiencies and be willing to make necessary adjustments so that the saints once again become the object of apostolic ministry, enabling them to effectively fulfill their purpose in the Kingdom of God.

I am aware that the traditional church does not lack voices speaking to these issues, but it does lack credible alternatives to the age-worn ways we continue to approach this critical training process. The Church was always meant to be a place of spiritual learning where the people of God receive training and are eventually allowed and expected to fulfill their personal ministries in the marketplace and through various secular activities. Somewhere along the way we adopted an ineffective plan, which places all ministry in the hands of a singular man. The "pastor" along with a staff of "spiritual specialists" is then expected to be the teacher, encourager, counselor and soul-winner while the **saints** play a rather sterile supporting role by faithfully offering their time, talent and treasure to various programs outlined by church leadership.

Paul, in his letter to the Ephesian church, stated that the apostle, prophet, evangelist, pastor and teacher were for the perfecting (maturing) of the **saints,** the work of the ministry (the ministry of the **saints**) and the edifying of the body of Christ (the **saints**). It is really all about the **saints.** I know it may be hard to believe but the New Testament was written to **saints,** not preachers. Ten of the New Testament books are directly addressed to the **saints** while the other books strongly infer the same. In short, the Church was to become a school (kindergarten, grade school, high school, college and graduate school) while the "five-fold" ministry serves as teachers and professors imparting the spiritual education necessary so that every believer becomes part of a great army called *The Ministry of the Saints.*

The Church must confront the need for change or risk the continuation of irrelevancy and ineffectiveness. Our present systems reek with insignificance and our stale approach to ministry is narrow and unscriptural. We change or we die. We proceed or the light that we have becomes darkness. With this in mind some of us really do not care about our precious reputations or religious correctness; we just want to see Christ's Kingdom come in the earth and are boldly proclaiming that the far-reaching vision of Daniel the prophet is to be fulfilled in our day.

*I beheld, and the same horn made war with the **saints**, and prevailed against them; Until the Ancient of days came, and judgment was given to the **saints** of the most High; and the time came that the **saints** possessed the kingdom.* Daniel 7:21-22

Dr. Mark Hanby
March 16, 2005

INTRODUCTION

Mark Twain described insanity as doing the same thing in the same way but expecting a different result. If that perception is correct, then perhaps the Church is manifesting signs of its own brand of insanity. This shadow of insanity is cast by a Church that continues to insist on laying the burden of ministry upon the shoulders of one man. This one-man approach to ministry has proven to be an ineffective style of accomplishing God's purposes in the world. The futility of this approach to ministry is reflected in the burnout among pastors and the frustration of God's people sitting in the pew. Nearing burnout, many pastors walk in disappointment wondering if there is a light on the other side of the tunnel. There is—it is the light of a multiplicity of ministry.

Christianity has long been waiting for the Church to enter a period of unprecedented revival and expecting the world to enter a great tribulation leading to the eventual appearing of Jesus Christ. For two millennia, the Church has been implementing the same methods built upon the same structures. They foolishly keep expecting God to bring forth a different result. Is it possible that this continued irrational approach has kept the Church from fulfilling its eternal purpose?

As pastors continue to live in despair and disillusionment and people leave the church in great numbers, is there any hope of change? I believe there is. There is a great move of the Spirit in our day that is declaring the Kingdom principles that were first announced by Jesus and manifested in the early Church. The establishment of these principles will lead to the founding of a Kingdom lifestyle or Kingdom culture.

These Kingdom principles can be broken down into four specific areas:

1. Kingdom Language: Just as French is spoken in France, so is the spiritual language of the Kingdom needed for communication and comprehension.

2. Kingdom Commerce: The ways of business and economic intercourse within the Kingdom.

3. Kingdom Protocol: The rules and manners pertaining to the order of the Kingdom.

4. Kingdom Government: The administration and rule of the Kingdom.

It is into this last category that multiplicity of ministry falls. Kingdom government is manifested through ministry. A properly ordered ministry will incorporate a multiplicity of ministry. Ministry that is not properly ordered will never bring forth Kingdom government. This book is an effort to describe and facilitate the establishment of a multiplicity of ministry.

For all our efforts and plans, the influence of Christianity in this generation has been on the decline. Not only has it not duplicated the power and spiritual manifestation of the first-century Church, but there is perhaps no period in the last two thousand years where the Church as a whole has been so ineffective in revealing a genuine Christ to the world. Perhaps it is time for the Church to ask itself some difficult but necessary questions.

Asking the Tough Questions

Although the Church has long been awaiting revival and the return of Jesus Christ, what if God is also waiting—waiting on His Church to first realign itself so that what He has spoken may come to pass? Maybe it is not a move of God we need, but a biblical reconfiguration of ministry? Maybe the Church needs a ministry ordered in a way that would allow the plan of God to come into its completion.

Is it possible regardless of all our good intentions and announcements of what the Lord is going to do, that the single most significant element of what God would do in His Church is dependent upon the restructuring of ministry according to biblical patterns?

It is quite likely that our focus has been misdirected. Perhaps we have been trying to furnish the house rather than instill the order for the proper assembling of the Church? Maybe the ministry has been focusing on form over substance? Or possibly we have been conditioned to live for the now rather than the future. It may even be possible that we've viewed God as the facilitator of our plans rather than the possessor of a magnificent plan that we are to complete. It is even conceivable that we have viewed Jesus as a heavenly Genie, rather than the goal and pursuit of our spiritual life.

In our fervor to do *a work* for God, is it at all remotely imaginable that we have largely failed in doing *the work* of God? It seems we have learned to fear evil rather than God. All too often we have exalted self over the Christ in us. Is it possible that the attention and praise of men have come at the expense of understanding God's clear plan, purpose, and order for His Church? In the following chapters, we will be examining present church structure and offering a biblical perspective of church government that is able to realign the Church with its purpose.

15

A Reordering of the Ministry

In the Book of First Samuel, Israel brought the ark of God, (a physical type of God and His presence), out of the tabernacle at Shiloh, never to return. For one hundred years, priests continued to minister according to their traditions in a place where God no longer resided. Then David in his hunger for God built a new place of worship, established a new order, and brought the ark back with him to Jerusalem. David reordered the priesthood according to a multiplicity of ministry. Likewise in our day, God is reordering His ministry to achieve the completion of His purpose.

For the church that is content to minister at the tabernacle in Shiloh, this text will be of little value. To those however who desire the prophetic fulfillment of David's tabernacle, who seek the perfection of the Lord's Church, this book offers a biblical understanding and plan to complete the New Testament government of the local church.

Perhaps at this point a cautionary statement is in order. What is contained herein will likely be determined, by those seeking comfort in the security of religious tradition, as a threat to that security. Fear of change can be so strong that it overpowers the soft consoling voice of the Spirit desiring us to come.

To many in the ministry, establishing a multiplicity of ministry entails more than finding the greater will of God or ordering the local church for its perfection. Many are concerned about their salaries, the security of pensions, and the likely loss of fellowship with those who may not understand or who might feel threatened by change. There is, however, a growing hunger within some of God's people overpowering the fear of man and seeking to find the order of God within ministry.

A Cry for Change

It seems that far too many writings attributed to Christian authorship are little more than skirmishes in a battle of opinions over who best hears and knows God the best. In our struggle to find the greater revelation of God's plan and purpose, we must not fall victim to placing ourselves in a position of judgment over God's people. Proper attitude is the single most important attribute in receiving greater understanding. Though it is God's prerogative to judge His people, we must each diligently seek out His plan and be willing to change when the light of His truth shines contrary to our traditions and opinions.

There is an increasing realization within the hearts of many that the religious structures of the present day will never bring the sought-after manifestation of God's Kingdom. We must confront the need for change or risk the continuation of irrelevancy and ineffectiveness. No longer content with the status quo, there is a rising tide among a remnant of God's people who are willing to bear any burden, pay any price, and endure any hardship that would establish the local church in His order and flood it with His purpose. It is for this latter group of spiritual sojourners that this book has been written.

The Glossary at the end of the book contains various ministry terms and an explanation of how they are used throughout this book. It might be good for you to familiarize yourself with these before proceeding.

———•••———

Chapter One

DEFINING MULTIPLICITY OF MINISTRY

Multiplicity of ministry is a multifaceted, many-sided ministry. It consists of many people, utilizing their various gifts and callings as they focus on a singularity of vision. The Church has a bank of human resources that is not being used to its fullest. The ministry of the Church needs to incorporate the many members of the Body if it is to truly be manifested in the world as the Body of Christ. If the perfection of the Church is ever to become a reality, the ministry of the Church cannot be the ministry of one man.

The prelude to the Kingdom will involve the reordering of the entire Body of Christ as to its ministry. Only ministry that is spawned out of the interaction and relationship of every member of the Body according to the unique gift, calling, and purpose of each, can be thought of as Kingdom ministry.

God is laying for us an immovable foundation of ministry. What we think of as a foundation is usually only the top of another's rubble. Ancient cities are often built upon the remains of previous inhabitants. Some scholars point to Jerusalem as being conquered over 40 times by invaders. Each time, a new city was built upon the remains of the previous disaster, thus it is common in many parts of the Holy City to dig through 60 feet or more of debris before reaching the original earth foundation.

Ministries likewise are often built upon foundations of previous spiritual disasters and failures, and tend to replicate the weaknesses of the old model rather than finding the solid footing of Kingdom ministry. Traditional understanding and application of ministry in the local church have hindered the manifestation of Kingdom ministry, found in a multiplicity of ministry.

We have, through tradition, defined the head of the local church as the *pastor*. In some church structures, he functions under the direction of a church board. In others, he is autonomous, operating at his own discretion. There are, of course, many denominational variations of local church organization. When speaking of the ministry of the local church, we are usually talking about the pastor.

The ministry of local church members (ushers, evangelism committees, prayer teams, music leaders, Sunday school teachers, etc.) are all included within this pastoral structure. Ministry of this type involves getting people into church and servicing their needs. Although these services are important, they generally limit the Spirit's ability to rule and govern sovereignly within the church.

We shall see, in future chapters, that a multiplicity of ministry is not only the New Testament plan for the organization of church ministry, but also has its pattern in the Old Testament as well. In seeking to establish this type of structure, it is important to understand that it is the only biblical plan for ensuring that the Holy Spirit has control of the local church to complete His purpose. In the traditional organization of ministry, an individual (usually a pastor), becomes the gatekeeper of the intention and movement of the Holy Spirit. In a multiplicity of ministry, the Holy Spirit truly becomes the sovereign of the Church.

Ministry Is Not Reserved for the Few

New Testament ministry is not an office but an expression of relationship each Christian has with the heavenly Father. The manifestation of the Spirit in and through every member of the Body for the completion of His purpose is the operation of true biblical ministry. Obedience to the Holy Spirit is the starting point of all ministry.

Ministry is not reserved for the few, for all of God's people are called to be ministers unto God. *"But ye are...a royal priest-hood"* (1 Pet. 2:9a)—not just some, but all in the Body are called to minister. Ministry is not about what we do to or for mankind, but about how we relate to our heavenly Father— being about our Father's business. *"Verily I say unto you, Inasmuch as ye have done it unto one of the least of these My brethren, ye have done it unto Me"* (Mt. 25:40b). God in His wisdom has determined that our ministry to Him is reflected in our ministry to each other and our fellowman as well.

The Tabernacle of David as a Transition Into a Multiplicity of Ministry

It is clear that we live in a time of transition as God is seeking by His Spirit to return the government of the Church back to those who understand the biblical patterns. David's tabernacle will give us insight into how to safely navigate through this paradigm shift. David revised and adjusted the government of His Kingdom bringing forth a new *pattern* of worship, a new *place* of worship, and a new *order* of ministry. These are a type of what the Spirit is doing today in the Church. This multiplicity of ministry is a part of the restored government God is bringing to the Church. David cried out to God, *"O God, Thou art my God; early will I seek Thee: my soul thirsteth for Thee, my flesh longeth for Thee in a dry and thirsty land, where no water is; to see Thy power and Thy glory, so as I have seen Thee in the sanctuary"* (Ps. 63:1-2). Hear David as he searches his mind for the mind of God: *"Lord, who shall abide in Thy tabernacle? who shall dwell in Thy holy hill?"* (Ps. 15:1)

David was after the heart of God! *"The humble shall see this, and be glad: and your heart shall live that seek God"* (Ps. 69:32); and again, *"Shall not God search this out? for He knoweth the secrets of the heart"* (Ps. 44:21).

David in his hunger for God would provide for a transition between the limitations and confines of an antiquated religious system represented by the tabernacle of Moses and the long, sought-after Kingdom. This former religious model of worship and ministry could never provide access for the heart that sought for the deeper things of God and the completion of destiny. The old religious system could bring people to God, but it could never bring them into God. Even though it at one time was sanctioned by God, it had outlived its purpose and would eventually be replaced by a new order of ministry and worship typified in David's tabernacle.

Moses' tabernacle and the ordinances performed therein were ordained by God. It was Moses' encounter with God on the mountain pertaining to the tabernacle and its ministry that occupies almost the whole of the last 15 chapters of Exodus. Yet, God in the day of the Philistines chose to leave this tabernacle, as evidenced by the ark of the covenant falling into the Philistines' hands, and dwell with the unbelievers rather than His own people. Israel had taken the presence of God for granted. They used this presence, typified by the ark of the covenant, as a religious charm to bring blessing but did not desire the presence of God in their hearts. By the time of Eli the priest, ministry and worship, fashioned around the tabernacle of Moses—was actually hindering Israel from having relationship with their God.

There was a transition time coming, leading to the establishment of David's tabernacle. In this tabernacle, the people of

Israel would have direct access to God aided by a priesthood who would facilitate this new order.

> *For the law having a shadow of good things to come, and not the very image of the things, can never with those sacrifices which they offered year by year continually make the comers thereunto perfect* (Hebrews 10:1).

Moses' tabernacle for the Jewish nation was the focal place of worship and the center for the offering of sacrifices under the law of Moses. It was at one time ordained of God and indeed, in type, has deep significance for the Church today; but as a method of ministry and worship, it had gone beyond its purpose. God was about to do a "new thing," but not all would immediately understand.

> *But now they desire a better country, that is, an heavenly: wherefore God is not ashamed to be called their God: for He hath prepared for them a city* (Hebrews 11:16).

David's tabernacle became the new order of ministry and worship displacing Moses' tabernacle. It speaks to us of a heavenly place. The only thing in David's tabernacle that was also in the former tabernacle was the ark of the presence of God. The traditions and furnishings of the previous tabernacle were variables and were no longer applicable to the present purpose of God.

God is always the constant and in the new tabernacle He was its center. In the ark He totally fulfilled the pattern of the furnishings of the tabernacle. Yet this new tabernacle of David would one day yield its divine ordained position to another tabernacle later known as Solomon's temple. Tents are temporary structures, and they are by design moveable. We must never stop or become so tied to past places, traditions, religious systems, and forms of ministry that we become incapable of moving after the wind of the Spirit.

The two tabernacles coexisted for one hundred years. While joyful worship, greater ministry, and divine liberty were being shared with God in David's tabernacle in Jerusalem, down in Shiloh priests were still offering sacrifices upon burnt altars and performing all sorts of cleansings and ceremonies. It was as though they did not recognize that the ark of God was no longer housed therein. God had departed from traditions and forms of ministry and worship He had once sanctioned and moved on; now He was doing a new thing. How sobering to think that our religious traditions and allegiance to past systems might hinder our ability to see and participate in the present move of God.

The church systems of our times are increasing in their insignificance as they continue to fail because of unproductive superstructures. The ministry organizations of the past will never bring forth the promised perfection of the Church. Only a multiplicity of ministry operating by the influence of every member of the Body of Christ will allow the domain of the King to be established throughout the world.

David had reordered the priesthood, provided for the participation of women in worship, erected a new tent in which the ark of God was not hid from the people, added music to worship, sought proper order of relationship, and brought the ark to Zion—all of which went against the old religious order. This was because he, being a man after God's own heart, desired relationship and love with God and desired God to be with the nation above all else. Although not welcomed by all, this was a new and deeper way of relating to God.

It is important to note that David did not command the removal of Moses' tabernacle in Shiloh. In fact, this tabernacle was to maintain a diminishing relevance in the history of Israel; and according to some historical accounts, its furnishings were eventually placed in a room under Solomon's temple. Those today who truly walk in the light of David's tabernacle will not seek to destroy the religious models of the past. We need to allow for a Holy Spirit transition from the old to the new. Moses' Tabernacle was based on a hierarchy of ministry, but in David's tabernacle we see bright appearances of a multiplicity of ministry.

Therefore the redeemed of the Lord shall return, and come with singing unto Zion; and everlasting joy shall be upon their head: they shall obtain gladness and joy; and sorrow and mourning shall flee away (Isaiah 51:11).

Zion the City of God

David rejoiced to bring the ark of God to Zion. All the people led by the king and priests, *in the correct order,* carried the ark of God's presence and placed it within a tent having one door. (Jesus is and always will be the only door.) They placed the ark on Mount Zion, a type of the city of God. Here all the people, governed by the priests, worshiped God.

"Ye are the light of the world. A city that is set on an hill cannot be hid" (Mt. 5:14). Jesus said the saints are a light and a city set on a hill. David brought the ark to the city and set it in God's place in the tent on Mount Zion. The ministry of the saints is the ministry of the city of God.

*And He said, Unto you it is given to know the mysteries of the kingdom of God: but to others in parables; that seeing they might not see, and hearing they might not understand. Now the parable is this: **The seed is the word of God*** (Luke 8:10-11, emphasis added).

*He answered and said unto them, He that soweth the good seed is the Son of man; the field is the world; **the good seed are the children of the kingdom;** but the tares are the children of the wicked one* (Matthew 13:37-38, emphasis added).

The seed that is the Word of God in the above Scripture in Luke is also the seed that is the children of God in Matthew. The Word of God that is the seed in the saints becomes the seed of the children of the Kingdom—the Word made flesh. Children of light manifest the Word of God. They are collectively, as the apostle Paul says, an epistle read of all men.

Mysteries are secrets of God, not kept from us, but rather kept for us. *"To whom God would make known what is the riches of the glory of this mystery among the Gentiles; which is Christ in you, the hope of glory"* (Col. 1:27).

The hope of the glory of God resides in Christ in His saints. The whole of the earth *"waiteth for the manifestation of the sons of God"* (Rom. 8:19b). These sons will be manifest as a city, a corporate man that will engage in the ministry of saints. *"For I would not, brethren, that ye should be ignorant of this mystery....There shall come out of Sion the Deliverer"* (Rom. 11:25-26a). This "Deliverer" is the many membered Body of Christ—Jesus is the head, and we are His Body.

"For God will save Zion...the seed also of His servants shall inherit it: and they that love His name shall dwell therein" (Ps. 69:35-36, emphasis added). This habitation of God spoken of in the tabernacle of David on Mount Zion is a type of the heavenly residence of the saints. "But ye are come unto mount Sion, and unto the city of the living God, the heavenly Jerusalem, and to an innumerable company of angels, to the general assembly and church of the firstborn, which are written in heaven, and to God the Judge of all, and to the spirits of just men made perfect" (Heb. 12:22-23).

The saints have more than a purpose; they have a destiny. Purpose is temporary; destiny is eternal. The purposes of God are eternal, but our purpose is not the same as our destiny. A door is important, and it has purpose. Who would want to own a house or drive a car without a door? A door provides security and controls access. It has purpose, but it does not have destiny. Destiny involves a destination.

Our destiny is to become a holy nation, the habitation of the Lord, a city set on a hill, a company of saints who reign and rule with Christ. We have an eternal destiny! *"...He shall come to be glorified in His saints, and to be admired in all them that believe (because our testimony among you was believed) in that day"* (2 Thess. 1:10). Jesus will be glorified in His Body.

We are a city set on a hill; we are Mount Zion. Is it possible we are the heavenly Jerusalem that comes down from God out of Heaven? Jesus will always be found in Jerusalem; it is the city of the great King. At 12 years old, Jesus was left in Jerusalem. He was not lost; He was ministering to the religious leaders, but Joseph and Mary did not know where to find Him.

They did what most in religion do—*"they sought Him among their kinsfolk and acquaintance"* (Lk. 2:44b). When the activity of life causes us to take our eyes off Jesus, we tend to look for Him in the traditions and religion of our lineage—kinfolk religion. He was not with relatives, but was where He had always been—in the temple in Jerusalem. They found Him after three days. If we allow Jesus to take us into the third dimension, we will find Him in our temple listening and giving answers to our questions and astonishing the fears within.

Oh that the salvation of Israel were come out of Zion! when the Lord bringeth back the captivity of His people, Jacob shall rejoice, and Israel shall be glad (Psalm 14:7).

...Behold, the Lord cometh with ten thousands of His saints, to execute judgment upon all, and to convince all that are ungodly among them of all their ungodly deeds which they have ungodly committed, and of all their hard speeches which ungodly sinners have spoken against Him (Jude 1:14-15).

And I looked, and, lo, a Lamb stood on the mount Sion, and with Him an hundred forty and four thousand, having His Father's name written in their foreheads (Revelation 14:1).

Him that overcometh will I make a pillar in the temple of My God, and he shall go no more out: and I will write upon him the name of My God, and the name of the city of My God, which is new Jerusalem, which cometh down out of heaven from My God: and I will write upon him My new name (Revelation 3:12).

Is it possible that the seed of God, which is the Word of God, will become the seed of God in His saints to bring forth the Kingdom? Is it also possible that as the saints of God are caught up to Him in revelation, they come down as a great city? Will the multiplicity of ministry within the saints of God ministering to the world be the salvation that comes forth from Zion? Is it possible that this is how the Lord will come in His saints to execute judgment and bring restoration?

Multiplicity Brings Multiplication

Multiplicity of ministry is also God's provision for the *multiplication* of ministry. Since ministry is multifaceted, the combination of many gifts and callings is necessary for the completion of any ministry vision. *"Now he that ministereth seed to the sower both minister bread for your food, and **multiply** your seed sown, and increase the fruits of your righteousness"* (2 Cor. 9:10, emphasis added). Various ministries working together will greatly multiply the effect of ministry.

With the apostle Paul's conversion and ministry in Jerusalem and the combined ministry of Ananias, Barnabas, and the apostles, a greater work was being accomplished. The brethren and Paul combined together in a multifaceted ministry that led to spiritual multiplication. Each executed a different and necessary facet of ministry through which the Spirit was able to complete His purpose. *"Then had the churches rest*

*throughout all Judaea and Galilee and Samaria, and were edified;
and walking in the fear of the Lord, and in the comfort of the Holy
Ghost, were **multiplied**"* (Acts 9:31, emphasis added).

> *Then the twelve called the multitude of the disciples unto
> them, and said, It is not reason that we should leave the
> word of God, and serve tables. Wherefore, brethren, look
> ye out among you seven men of honest report, full of the
> Holy Ghost and wisdom, whom we may appoint over this
> business. But we will give ourselves continually to prayer,
> and to the ministry of the word.... Whom they set before
> the apostles: and when they had prayed, they laid their
> hands on them. And the word of God increased; and the
> number of the disciples **multiplied** in Jerusalem...* (Acts
> 6:2-4,6-7, emphasis added).

In Acts chapter 6, the ministry of the apostles was being
hindered. Subsequently, the decision by the apostles to introduce
certain spiritual men into various facets of the work lessened the
load the apostles carried and resulted in a multiplication of effective ministry. *Multiplicity of ministry is not just about getting people to
help the pastor with his vision.* It is about allowing the Holy Spirit
to establish biblical order within ministry so that the Spirit can
be manifested through a variety of people. This spiritual order
will bring into play the necessary parts for the completion of a
particular ministry.

In the above events, the Holy Spirit helped the young
Church understand that ministry belonged to all. The early
Church had been using the Jewish church as a pattern wherein
ministry was vested in a religious hierarchy. But by the time of
the writing of the Pauline Epistles, the fivefold ministry to the
saints and the ministry of saints to the world had become an
expanding practice.

It became apparent that in order for the work of the Spirit
to multiply, a multifaceted ministry would need to be adopted.
This eventually led to a focus in which every prepared saint of

God had spiritual employment. Ministry was not just for a few, but for everyone, according to their gifting, calling, preparation, ability, and availability.

It's About Alignment

In the past, many have thought God's work was dependent upon their Bible knowledge, personal sacrifice, and their commitment to fasting, prayer, and good deeds. They were convinced that these religious activities would demonstrate how much they really desired "revival." This religious misconception is spawned by a lack of understanding concerning how the will of God is accomplished.

For ever, O Lord, Thy word is settled in heaven (Psalm 119:89).

For we which have believed do enter into rest, as He said, As I have sworn in My wrath, if they shall enter into My rest: although the works were finished from the foundation of the world (Hebrews 4:3).

Everything that God has done or is going to do has already been accomplished in Heaven. His will is completed in Heaven. *"Thy kingdom come. Thy will be done in earth, as it is in heaven"* (Mt. 6:10). Spiritual alignment is the operation of the Spirit whereby what is finished in Heaven is brought to pass in the earth.

It is in earth as it is in Heaven. Not just in *the* earth, but in *our* earth. We are made of the elements of the earth. Our success in God is not determined by our knowledge, office, or gifting alone, but by our order. God is quite capable of doing what is necessary. However, He is looking for willing vessels—meaning *obedient*—who will allow His order to fashion their vessels so that the Holy Spirit will have freedom to do His will.

Alignment is about positioning ourselves in the plan and purpose of God so that in His sovereignty He brings His will to pass. It is not about my abilities and knowledge, but about His will and power. Ministries that are out of alignment depend upon the fruit of their own hands accomplished through their gifting and abilities. Instead of giving glory to the Lord, they seek and receive recognition and glory for themselves and their own efforts. *"They worship the work of their own hands, that which their own fingers have made"* (Is. 2:8b).

Misalignment Causes Pain and Restricts Proper Movement

All things that function properly in the natural world are in full alignment. It is the things that are out of alignment that cause pain and restrict proper operation. For example, the vertebras of the human back, if properly aligned, are able to accommodate graceful ballet movements as well as withstand tremendous stress loads. Yet, if only one vertebra is not properly aligned, it can cause great pain and impede movement.

Body movement is not hindered because of some problem with the brain, but because the misalignment of the vertebra will not allow it to function properly. Likewise, in the Church, it is often not about what the Lord wills to do, but about whether or not ministry is in proper alignment so that it can function according to the will of the Lord.

Alignment allows us to enter the rest of God. The weight of the work is no longer placed inappropriately on the shoulder of just one person. As we cease from our own poorly devised plans and reposition the ministry on the whole Body, then we will see the manifestation of God's will on the earth. We will replace sweat with rest, resulting in a dynamic release of the whole Body into the work of the Lord, which will affect the culture around us. Things in our ministries, already completed in the heavens and finished from the foundation of the world, will come to pass—not because of our efforts, but because we are aligned with His Spirit and His purposes. Proper alignment of ministry in the local church will be realized when we commit ourselves to a multiplicity of ministry.

Chapter Two

———•·••·•———

PREREQUISITES FOR ESTABLISHING A MULTIPLICITY OF MINISTRY

If the Church is going to successfully establish a *multiplicity of ministry*, then she must understand and be aware of certain critical conditions. It is essential that the leaders in the Church do not arbitrarily seek to implement change until they understand these foundational requirements.

Prerequisite #1: Father/Son Order

A multiplicity of ministry can only become properly instituted within a church that is in father/son order. The order of ministry in the Bible was always from father to son. Unless we are connected to a ministry father, we have no biblical right to ministry or to foster ministry sons.

In recent years as the truth of father/son order has permeated various Christian circles, many counterfeits have arisen. Father/son order is not about having a human mediator, a spiritual coach, or even a mentor. Unfortunately, many have taught a perversion of this order in an effort to increase personal control or gain financial advantage instead of extending their heavenly vision through successive generations.

The order of God within His Kingdom is the order of father to son. If we are ever to find our way out of religious

Babylon (confusion), the Church must discover the ministry order of the Kingdom. The present church system is patterned after political, social, and business models of man and not after the biblical order. Leadership is chosen via a voting process or by an in-house promotion system and not according to proper order. As a result, authority doesn't flow from God, but from man.

Proper father/son order is a requirement for implementing a multiplicity of ministry. The book, *You Have Not Many Fathers,* by Mark Hanby, is a valuable resource for understanding and establishing father/son order within a church.

Prerequisite #2: A Church Founded on Set Ministry

In each local church that is in proper order, God has set a minister to establish and oversee the work. This minister, usually called the pastor, is not the owner of the church. He is not necessarily the wisest or most spiritual of all the members in the congregation. In fact, the pastor's spiritual gifting in certain areas may not even approach that of many in the faithful sainthood; however, his position of authority is ordained by God.

The set minister cannot be all things to all people; he must not view himself or be viewed as the repository of all knowledge or the one who has the answer to every need in every situation. He is, however, the only one, because of the position entrusted to his care, who can minister an order which will complete God's vision for a particular local body.

In his position as the set minister, he must institute proper order to establish and oversee the work of the local church. More than any other single task, it is bringing the church into proper father/son order that must define his ministry. Ministries without divine order tend to define themselves by size, influence, or gifting.

Ministerial **respon**sibility is the ability to provide proper response to those issues related to our ministries. The difference between reacting to a situation and responding to one can be vast. When someone reacts, he allows circumstances to dictate his actions and attitudes; when someone responds, he allows his attitudes and actions to be controlled by an ordered and developed character. This is a significant factor in being effective in ministry.

Many in ministry find themselves constantly reacting to "problems." Sometimes a minister may find himself in the position of continually putting out fires within the church. No sooner does he deal with one situation than another arises. This creates a position of stress that opposes the peace of God.

The ministry oftentimes finds itself continually reacting (having to act again), because it defaults in its responsibility to set proper father/son order throughout the generations of the church. Learning to respond and establishing an order within the church that allows response to the Spirit rather than reaction to opposition is one of the primary responsibilities of the set ministry.

Set ministry is a ministry of leadership. Set ministry knows its destiny and purpose and is able to define it as a clear godly vision that directs the church. It is responsible for the effective operation of the church and establishes the church upon the government of God and not upon that of man. Set ministry is responsible for how and what the church is taught, which requires sound doctrine and grounding in the truth.

Set ministry is responsible for the training of ministry and the completion of church order, which requires the establishment of biblical father/son order. It is also responsible for accommodating the ministry and move of the Spirit throughout the Body, which requires the establishment of a multiplicity of ministry.

And God hath set some in the church, first apostles, secondarily prophets, thirdly teachers, after that miracles, then gifts of healings, helps, governments, diversities of tongues (1 Corinthians 12:28).

It is God who sets ministry within a church. This does not come by the voting or appointment of men. In the setting of this ministry, there is an order: *first... secondly... thirdly... after that.* The apostolic will always be first. We will see in a subsequent chapter that whether the set ministry has a teacher gifting, a prophetic gifting, or some other gifting, as set ministry they do the work of an apostle. They are the ones set in a specific place to lay foundations and establish the work for which God has called them.

But now hath God set the members every one of them in the body, as it hath pleased Him (1 Corinthians 12:18).

God sets both the ministry and the members of the Body. If churches better understood this fact, they would not be so eager to gather anyone they could into their midst, but would look for those whom the Lord has brought for His purpose. It is a surprise to many pastors that not everyone belongs in their church. The reason this is not usually understood is because few local churches have the ministry order or biblical vision that would make this apparent. The ministry and the people are frustrated because the church is not in proper order.

Attracting Church Members

Most churches to do not teach those seeking prospective membership how to properly look for a local church. Churches often think and act with a department store mentality looking to attract customers. "We have the best music, anointed preaching, a beautiful building, great activities for all ages—please come and join us. You'll be glad you did!" Some are so hungry for warm bodies to fill the pews and add funding to the coffers that they are willing to, and indeed do, seek anyone who will agree to a few minimal requests. This is called "saving the lost and ministering to their need."

Has the average church even considered the possibility that not everyone belongs in their specific local church? Does not God have a unique call and purpose for each local church? Can there be some people who He would send to one church that He may not send to another?

Are not specific people sent to a certain local church dependent upon God's purpose and the vision of that church? There is a place in God's Church for every hungering person, but does He indiscriminately assign people to local churches without taking into account His purpose for them and His vision for the Body? Is it God or man who adds to the Church? Of course, if a local church does not have a well-defined vision, how would it know who should be part of the work?

Religion has often made it easy to enter the church but difficult to leave. Would it not be better for it to be difficult to enter and easy to leave? By being difficult to enter, we are not speaking about being exclusive or putting extensive demands upon people seeking a church. Rather, we are referring to giving them a proper understanding about the purpose and vision of the local church and teaching them how to allow the Spirit to direct them into their place and purpose.

Let the Lord, the God of the spirits of all flesh, set a man over the congregation (Numbers 27:16).

Moses understood that God sets the ministry over the people. The one who was to take the place of Moses was Joshua, Moses' ministry son. Joshua was someone on whom Moses could place a portion of his spirit. This is an example of generational ministry.

If set ministry is primarily concerned about its own ministry, it will force the saints to become servants to the pastor, rather than helping the saints find and develop their ministry. This is why most pastorates never become generational. In other words, their vision (if they have one) for the most part ends with their leaving. If, however, they have raised ministry sons, then those sons will be able to carry on the vision. The church then has the potential to become a spiritual family and not just a gathering of like-minded people who love Jesus.

Israel hath cast off the thing that is good: the enemy shall pursue him (Hosea 8:3).

For this cause left I thee in Crete, that thou shouldest set in order the things that are wanting, and ordain elders in every city, as I had appointed thee (Titus 1:5).

Set ministry establishes order and ordains local leadership. The hand of God through Paul set Titus over the work in Crete to bring order to the church. We have no biblical record that the apostle Paul was ever in Colosse, and only a brief account of an unplanned visit to Crete, yet the rule of his ministry spread to these and other places primarily because of his ministry sons.

And the rest will I set in order when I come (1 Corinthians 11:34b).

Paul was the set ministry over the churches entrusted into his care. As such, he established and maintained order in those settings. It was not by virtue of his education, denominational affiliation, or by the election of the local church membership that he held his authority to rule in these churches—he was ordained by God.

But contrariwise, when they saw that the gospel of the uncircumcision was committed unto me (Galatians 2:7a).

Beside those things that are without, that which cometh upon me daily, the care of all the churches (2 Corinthians 11:28).

If I be not an apostle unto others, yet doubtless I am to you: for the seal of mine apostleship are ye in the Lord (1 Corinthians 9:2).

As set ministry over certain locals, Paul exercised rule. This rule cannot be granted by man or obtained through education, but only comes from the Lord. Many in ministry exert authority over others by virtue of the office they hold, but only set ministry in proper order can fully exercise the measure of rule given by the Spirit and extend that rule to sons.

Prerequisite #3: Proper Vision

The importance of a well-defined ministry vision from God cannot be overstated. It is essential. It is impossible to give clear godly direction to a local church without proper ministry vision. If the set ministry cannot see the vision of the Lord for their settings, they will never be able to complete ministry or pass on inheritance.

Lack of biblical vision is why so many ministers stay in the pulpit until they die or retire. Because they do not have a proper ministry vision, they are never quite sure when or if their ministry is completed. If a ministry does not have a clear vision, it cannot say what is required to complete that vision. In order to have a proper ministry vision, a ministry father is needed from whom vision can be drawn and then that vision should be passed onto others.

In organizational structures, a proper ministry vision is not required because the propagation and control of the organization become the vision and its implementation. In the case of independent churches, the doctrine and aspirations of the pastor often become the vision. This is why most churches state their vision in broad and unspecific terms such as "God has called us to bring the gospel to this city," or "The Lord will use us as a refuge for the lost and a ministry to reach the world." These are nice sentiments and may even be promises from God, but these types of statements are not ministry visions.

Not having a well-defined ministry vision from God is fiduciary evidence that the direction of the work is from man and not God. According to church growth specialists, among the top reasons for joining a local church are: location, preaching abilities of the pastor, family programs, amenities of the church facilities, similarities to other churches attended, and doctrinal beliefs.

Many people use these criterion in choosing a church, but there are others of far greater importance. For example: "What is the vision of this church, and is God's voice is speaking to me in agreement with that vision?" It is proper vision that brings unity, purpose, direction, and ministry. We can gather people together for all sorts of peripheral reasons, but only proper ministry vision can provide the suitable foundation for connecting Christians in a local body.

Prerequisite #4: Understanding the Corporate Body

There is a misconception in much of Christianity that God deals primarily with individuals—His highest purpose being to save individuals from their sin. Although He desires to save individuals, it is really the salvation and manifestation of His Body or the corporate man that is in the ultimate purpose of God. "Salvation" carried to the entire world requires this manifestation. Without understanding the corporate man, it is impossible to comprehend ministry or what the Lord is doing in our day. Consequently, many people think that God's purpose today is for His Church to reach as many lost souls as possible before the rapture and horrendous unleashing of the tribulation upon the earth. They have never understood that what God is doing in this day is not found in His desire to release wrath on the earth but in bringing forth the manifestation of His Body—the new man. Jesus cannot return without the manifestation of His Body. The ministry of the corporate man can essentially be accomplished only through a multiplicity of ministry.

> *And thou shalt say unto Pharaoh, Thus saith the Lord, Israel is My son, even My firstborn* (Exodus 4:22, emphasis added).

> *For unto which of the angels said He at any time, Thou art My Son, this day have I begotten thee? And again, I will be to him a Father, and he shall be to Me a Son?* (Hebrews 1:5, emphasis added)

> *He that overcometh shall inherit all things; and I will be his God, and he shall be My son* (Revelation 21:7, emphasis added).

God's dealing with man is progressive and corporate. God dealt with Israel—not just Israelites; likewise, God deals with the Church—not just saints, and God will deal with those who are "the Christ"—not just Christians. The ministry and purpose of God to man is always from a father to a son and is progressive and corporate.

> *Israel hath sinned, and they have also transgressed My covenant* (Joshua 7:11a).

> *The Lord said also unto me...Hast thou seen that which backsliding Israel hath done?* (Jeremiah 3:6a)

> *Israel hath cast off the thing that is good: the enemy shall pursue him* (Hosea 8:3).

He is not just the God of the Israelites, but also the God of Israel; and in His plan, He deals with them corporately and not individually. Individually, there were Israelites who followed God as well as those who turned from Him, but God dealt with Israel corporately. In our day, He continues to deal with His people corporately, something much of the Church has yet to understand.

When Adam, the son of God (see Lk 3:38), sinned, God gathered a people, the Israelites, under the law, and called them, "My son." Salvation (that the law could not bring because of the weakness of flesh) was brought to man through another Son of God. God called Jesus, "My Son" when Jesus was brought forth into ministry. Jesus saved mankind, but it will be another son, whom Jesus calls, "My son" (see Rev. 21:7), who will manifest in earth the salvation and manifestation of the Savior.

A multiplicity of ministry will only make sense to those who understand that God's dealing with man in this day is corporate.

*And have put on the **new man**, which is renewed in knowledge after the image of Him that created him: where there is neither Greek nor Jew, circumcision nor uncircumcision, Barbarian, Scythian, bond nor free: but **Christ is all**, and in all (Colossians 3:10-11, emphasis added).*

*Having abolished in His flesh the enmity, even the law of commandments contained in ordinances; for to make in Himself of twain **one new man**, so making peace (Ephesians 2:15, emphasis added).*

*And He gave some, apostles; and some, prophets; and some, evangelists; and some, pastors and teachers; for the perfecting of the saints, for the work of the ministry, for the edifying of the body of Christ: till we all come in the unity of the faith, and of the knowledge of the Son of God, **unto a perfect man**, unto the measure of the stature of the fulness of Christ: that we henceforth be no more children, tossed to and fro, and carried about with every wind of doctrine, by the sleight of men, and cunning craftiness, whereby they lie in wait to deceive; but speaking the truth in love, may grow up into Him in all things, which is the head, even Christ: from whom the whole body fitly joined together and compacted by that which every* *joint supplieth, according to the effectual working in the measure of every part, **maketh increase of the body unto the edifying of itself** in love* (Ephesians 4:11-16, emphasis added).

It is the Lord, who is Jesus, and His Christ, who is the corporate man, the new man who will manifest Jesus. The Lord and His Christ will rule the Kingdom.

The saints are the Christ (anointed) of God. We are to be the Body of Christ or Christ's Body with Jesus as the head. We are anointed ones (Christs) who manifest the head to all the world.

*The kings of the earth stood up, and the rulers were gathered together against the Lord [Jesus], and against **His Christ** [the corporate man]* (Acts 4:26, emphasis added).

*And the seventh angel sounded; and there were great voices in heaven, saying, The kingdoms of this world are become the kingdoms of our Lord, and of **His Christ**; and He shall reign for ever and ever* (Revelation 11:15, emphasis added).

*And I heard a loud voice saying in heaven, Now is come salvation, and strength, and the kingdom of our God, and the power of **His Christ**: for the accuser of our brethren is cast down, which accused them before our God day and night* (Revelation 12:10, emphasis added).

This new man, the corporate man is manifested as the Body of Christ—not individually as Christians, but corporately as a singular Body. *"Til we all come...unto a perfect man"*; **we** (plural) become **a** (singular) man. The order of ministry within this Body is from father to son and is a multiplicity of ministry. If we understand ministry only in an individual context, rather than corporately, we will never implement a multiplicity of ministry which is the Kingdom order of ministry.

*There is **one body**, and one Spirit, even as ye are called in one hope of your calling* (Ephesians 4:4, emphasis added).

But now are they many members, yet but one body (1 Corinthians 12:20, emphasis added).

Chapter Three

PREPARATION FOR ESTABLISHING A MULTIPLICITY OF MINISTRY

Those "in ministry" may at times feel the loneliness of the call, the frustration of the work, or sense a great personal lack in regard to the task set before them. A large part of our confusion lies in our perception that the struggle of process is of the enemy and consider only the blessing to be of God. Furthermore, we interpret blessing to be anything that achieves our goal or desire in the work of God, never realizing that our goal or desire may not be His.

We often define that which causes struggle as being contrary to the fulfillment of our goals and desires, and therefore of the enemy. We have not properly considered that struggle and affliction could be sanctioned by God and be of far greater value in His purpose than the end for which we look. Our struggles, obstacles, and frustrations, our fears, discouragements, and oppositions are most likely working for us, not against us. They all work toward the moment—the time in which God resets our spiritual clocks—and old things give way to the new.

For our light affliction, which is but for a moment, worketh for us a far more exceeding and eternal weight of glory (2 Corinthians 4:17).

Understanding That the Reward Is in the Process

God is not result oriented but process oriented. He has already determined the outcome and settled His Word in the heavens. It is not a question of if His will shall be done, but how and by whom. He is seeking obedience, not sacrifice. Therefore, His focus is not like ours. We see a task, and we look for its completion. We have a church building to finish, pews to fill, or a mission to establish. We see the blessing of God only in our ability to fulfill the desire we think is His will.

In God, process and result are inextricably linked to each other. He is process oriented. Each step along the road to our development is as important to God as the final result. He is not only looking to achieve some ultimate purpose but also to have the pattern of Christ formed within each of us. This requires constant, as well as Spirit-measured, change within each of us.

God sees the end from the beginning; He sees in whole and not just in part. God sees the fulfillment of His will in the sanctification of our souls through process leading to our establishment in Christ.

> *Remember the former things of old: for I am God, and there is none else; I am God, and there is none like Me, declaring the end from the beginning, and from ancient times the things that are not yet done, saying, My counsel shall stand, and I will do all My pleasure* (Isaiah 46:9-10).

If we as ministry desire to establish God's order within our settings (a multiplicity of ministry), we need to first have a clear vision of what it is that He would have us do. Our organization and planning mean little if what we are planning for is not fully in the purpose of God. If our planning is only for what we think He would have us do, we may find that after years of labor we have endured great and unnecessary frustration. Our frustration may not be in doing the will of the Lord but as a result of trying to achieve our own agendas that we assumed were the will of the Lord.

Everything in our ministries must be put on trial for its life to test whether these things be of God or rooted in our own desire. We need to stop doing everything the Lord never told us to do, even good things, but things nevertheless that are at variance with His plan for us. This is necessary so that our desire is not in conflict with His purpose. We must learn to let the Spirit lead us past our ministerial aspirations and into His perfect will.

To do this we are required to ask the right questions: Did God tell me to do this? How do I know He told me to do this? Am I gauging my understanding of His will on what I desire to see and not on what I know? Am I applying ministry out of my traditions and habits? Have we done some things for so long that the very longevity and acceptance by others proves their validity to us? How is this fulfilling the vision given to me?

Sometimes Even Mighty Apostles Have a Difficult Time Hearing God

As the most heralded of the original twelve apostles, Peter and his relationship with Jesus has inspired a multitude of sermons. He is always given first position in the listing of the apostles, having been with Jesus at the times of His greatest miracles, and given charge by Jesus to the keys of the Kingdom.

Peter was a great apostle and the keynote speaker at the birthday of the Church. He was beaten and thrown in jail for giving supremacy to the voice of the Spirit over the voice of men, and on one occasion he was even freed from prison and saved from death through a mighty angelic miracle.

The power of God flowed mightily and miraculously in this vessel, so much so, that the casting of his shadow healed multitudes. This was no mere saint, but a mighty spiritual warrior sold out for the message of the cross. But even the great apostle Peter had to learn an important spiritual principle—everything in ministry must be put on trial for its life.

In the will of God, salvation included not only the Jews but also the Gentiles. This was a startling prospect not only for Peter but also for the entire Christian community at the time of Acts chapter 10. Peter had a deep relationship with Jesus and was mightily used of God. He could not, however, see past his tradition, assumptions, and prejudices. He had a difficult time seeing that salvation was also for the Gentiles and an even harder time convincing the Church. In fact, there were some of the circumcision who never would be convinced.

It took a powerful vision, angelic intervention, and supernatural acts of the Holy Spirit to change his ministry. In stating his case before the elders of the Church in Jerusalem, Peter answered their skepticism by asking the question, *"What was I, that I could withstand God?"* (Acts 11:17b)

It was one thing to believe that Gentiles could be saved; it was another to overcome the prejudice of others and the need to be accepted by peers. In Galatians chapter 2, Paul corrected Peter to his face. Peter was willing to eat with Gentiles as long as no Jewish Christians were present; but when certain Jews came down from Jerusalem to Antioch, he separated himself and would eat only with the Jews.

God had Peter put everything on trial for its life. To Peter's credit, he was willing to change. Though it no doubt meant certain criticism by some of the circumcision, he yielded to the voice of God.

Peter had to allow God to put his most fervently held beliefs on trial for their life. He allowed process to bring forth God's intended result. When ministry is unwilling to do likewise, it impedes its own future. Our religious traditions, training, and biases withstand the will of God. Ministry desiring

God's fullness must allow what it has come to understand about the order of ministry, formed by religious doctrines, to be put on trial in the heavenly court.

Understanding and implementing a multiplicity of ministry requires change. As with Peter and the Jerusalem Church, God is performing mighty acts for ministry and His present-day Church to bring forth His ministry order. Those willing to allow God to put their heartfelt beliefs and unrecognized prejudices on trial will find the will of God as it relates to the multiplicity of ministry.

Foundation or Substructure of Ministry

It should be obvious to all that ministry needs to be established upon proper foundation. One of the greatest mistakes comes in trying to build without proper foundation. And, of course, this mistake can be made in the church as easily as it is made in individual lives. Failure in ministry is almost always related to improper or unsuitable foundations.

The problem is that the weakness is often not visible until what is built begins to crumble. By this time, it is usually too late to redo the substructure. Ministries become obsessed with trying to hold on to things they've worked so hard to acquire, often spending years trying to shore up crumbling works rather than establishing proper foundation.

In the late 1940's, the White House, after 138 years of continuous use, fell into a serious state of deterioration. Architectural engineers advised a complete overhaul of the substructure of the building in order to prevent its collapse. In an effort to save as much of this historically significant building as possible, the house was disassembled one piece at a time. Sections of plaster, moldings, wood flooring, exterior stonework—in fact, every part of the building was numbered and charted so that as much as possible of the building could be reassembled using original components.

A larger basement was then dug with a new concrete foundation and a steel substructure installed. To this substructure was painstakingly added the disassembled pieces of the original building. The White House was preserved, and its utility was increased by the provision of a proper foundation.

This is similar to present-day churches that have put extensive time and commitment into building a religious façade, portraying what they deem to be a beautiful exterior to the public but giving little if any attention to the substructure. Without proper foundation, no work of ministry will last.

Of course, if a ministry is concerned only with what happens during its own lifetime, proper foundation will have little importance. The same curse of immaturity in modern society is a curse in the Church as well. An immature church lives in single portions of God's purpose and power rather than in the double portions of the generational blessing.

We are living in a hurry-up, me-first, money-driven society where value is measured by a monetary rather than a character-based standard. Integrity is seldom as important as financial profit, and process is rarely valued as highly as reward. The Church, likewise, is not interested in that which may upset its traditions or survive past this present generation.

The quest in much of ministry for larger churches, broader platforms, wider recognition, financial extravagance, and the perpetuating of ill-conceived and spiritually harmful dogmas and traditions is easily recognized by the world for what it is. Many in the world recognize the need and hypocrisy of the Church, to be little different from what they experience in daily life. Ministry that is lacking proper foundation will be ill-focused. The Church may be blind, but it has not escaped the watchful eye of the world.

This is why so much of ministry is confused, hurting, seeking meaning and purpose. Those who attempt to tell the world that purpose, peace, and meaning are to be found in Jesus often have great difficulty in securing these same things from Him. Because they have no proper foundation, their ministries are greatly shaken when the blessings of the world they hunger for, (large followings, abundant finances, religious influence, etc.), become jeopardized or unattainable. Unlike the renovation of the White House, in ministry it is almost impossible to save the desired facade while foundations are rebuilt.

What Is the Foundation?

For other foundation can no man lay than that is laid, which is Jesus Christ (1 Corinthians 3:11).

Jesus, of course, is the foundation; but what does that mean exactly? In religious understanding, we would take that to mean that He is the one who our life and salvation are built upon, and this, of course, is true; but beyond that, He has given us a clear pattern for implementing this truth within the Church. The Church, for the most part, has only superficially understood this foundation, and consequently, has had to discover and seek to reproduce in each generation *"things kept secret from the foundation of the world."* (Matthew 13:35, emphasis added).

For when for the time ye ought to be teachers, ye have need that one teach you again which be the first principles of the oracles of God; and are become such as have need of milk, and not of strong meat. For every one that useth milk is unskilful in the word of righteousness: for he is a babe. But strong meat belongeth to them that are of full age, even those who by reason of use have their senses exercised to discern both good and evil. Therefore leaving the principles of the doctrine of Christ, let us go on unto perfection; not laying again the foundation of repentance from dead works, and of faith toward God, of the doctrine of baptisms, and of laying on of hands, and of resurrection of the dead, and of eternal judgment. And this will we do, if God permit. For it is impossible for those who were once enlightened, and have tasted of the heavenly gift, and were made partakers of the Holy Ghost, and have tasted the good word of God, and the powers of the world to come, if they shall fall away, to renew them again unto repentance; seeing they crucify to themselves the Son of God afresh, and put Him to an open shame (Hebrews 5:12–6:6).

Saints should be the teachers of men, but because of the immaturity and disorder in ministry, they have a need to be taught "first principles" again. The Church has only been able to handle instruction fit for children, and not teaching that requires maturity. The writer of Hebrews explains that, for the Church to go on to its destiny (perfection), it must get beyond foundation principles. Christ is the foundation, and that one foundation is found in six areas that must be completed in order to go on to perfection (meaning, maturity, completion, wholeness).

If the Church does not desire perfection or aspire to its destiny of becoming the manifested Body of Christ, there is no reason for it to establish proper foundation. This foundation in large part is not being put within the saints because the disorder in ministry does not allow for either the saints' or the ministries' maturation.

There are six aspects to the one foundation: repentance from dead works, faith toward God, doctrine of baptisms, laying on of hands, resurrection from the dead, and eternal judgment. Why can't the Church go on to perfection? Simply, it doesn't have a proper foundation. An out-of-order ministry can only pass on its immaturity to the saints rather than the meat of the Word that would bring the saints and the Church into proper ministry.

The six aspects of the one foundation are generally taught and understood as "milk doctrines," meaning they are basic doctrines to be understood by young Christians. The limited depth of perception of dimensional truth has hindered many churches from laying even basic foundations. Instead of going on to perfection and maturity, some make these foundations their destination for Kingdom possibility and purpose.

If the foundations be destroyed, what can the righteous do? (Psalm 11:3)

The Church has trouble establishing order because its foundations are so weak. A multiplicity of ministry must be built on a mature foundation. To establish biblical foundation, ministry must first desire to come into order.

To those who have their senses exercised, these six aspects of the foundations of Christ have far more significance than as described above. Foundation suitable to hold the perfection of the saints requires a higher understanding. There is an order to this foundation, and it is progressive; it is briefly stated as follows:

Repentance From Dead Works

Repentance from dead works is a change from religious works. Religion holds God's people in bondage and often brings spiritual death. Just as Pharaoh set taskmasters over the Israelites to divide them from their God by their works, so does religion. To progress in God, His people must first be set free from the bondage of religion. This is the work of righteousness. See Exodus 5, Isaiah 32:17, and Matthew 6:33.

Faith Toward God

Faith toward God is submission toward the vision. After the saints mature past the bondage of religion, their faith toward God leads them to follow after vision. It is faith toward God. It has direction. Only proper vision allows a church to see what God sees and to complete the will of God on the earth as it is in the heavens. This faith allows ministry to see what God sees. See Romans 3:1-31; 9:28-32.

Doctrine of Baptisms

Doctrine of baptisms is the initiation into dimensions. The baptisms of water, spirit, and fire correspond to the initiation into the three dimensions of grace as typified in the tabernacle of Moses. Once saints are set free of religious bondage and connected to the vision of God, they then can see that God's plan for the Church and for their lives is progressive, (meaning dimensional). He never meant for us to get saved, sit on a church pew, and invite others to wait with us for the rapture. He has a great plan for us leading to our perfection. Only an understanding of this dimensional pattern will lead us to maturity in Christ. See Second Corinthians 1:10; Second Thessalonians 5:23; and Titus 3:5.

Laying on of Hands

Laying on of hands is the government of God in ministry order. When the saints understand there is a dimensional order in God and that His purpose for them goes far beyond initial salvation, then coming under the authority of the government of God is not a strain, but a desire. Government is the vehicle for dispensing God's authority in the Church. The hand is a type of the ministry of God. Ministry is not self-appointed but comes through the laying on of hands. A ministry father must lay his hands on a ministry son (meaning, sanction the son's ministry), if the son is to be in order. A multiplicity of ministry, being the order of God for the Church, is an important vehicle of ministerial impartation. A Church in proper ministry order is foundational. See Numbers 27:18-23; Matthew 9:18; Acts 8:18; and First Timothy 4:14.

Resurrection From the Dead

Resurrection from the dead is the process of God taking us from death to life. Man sinned and death entered into the world. The reversal of the curse will bring forth eternal life in every dimension. A Church that is set free from religion, understands and follows vision, knows its purpose in the progressive will of God, and is under governmental order, will begin to reverse the curse of death. This Church will not focus on hell, death, and punishment, but on the reestablishment of eternal life (spiritually, physically, emotionally, mentally, and universally). See John 11:17-26; First Corinthians 15; John 14:1-6; First John 5:20; and Jude 1:21.

Eternal Judgment

Eternal Judgment is the establishment of the corporate man in Christ. Eternal judgment is usually taught as a negative thing. Actually, it is a very positive and good thing. God has a judgment that is eternal. He has already and eternally judged sin. He has already established that righteousness shall reign. The prince of this world is already and eternally judged. See Second Thessalonians 1:4-5; First John 4:17; Hebrews 4:3; John 16:11; and Jude 1:15.

Foundation of Ministry

Proper establishment of this six-part foundation is a requirement if the Church is to go on to perfection.

The foundation is the underlying structure that gives form and strength to all that is attached to it or placed on it. The construction of great skyscrapers of one hundred or more stories is possible because a proper foundation of steel and concrete enables the building to withstand tremendous loads and stresses. Without this steel substructure, a building would be little more than a pile of brick, wire, wood, carpet, and piping—valuable but unable to complete its intended purpose.

The human skeleton gives shape and protection to our body and allows it to function and move. Without this foundation of bones and joints, the brain and all the intricate organs, vessels, and muscular wonders of the body would be nothing more than a blob of tissue unable to complete its function. Ministry likewise can never function properly if it is not built upon an appropriate foundation.

The human skeleton and the substructure of a skyscraper are for the most part hidden. We tend to give far more attention to the visible attributes of the body or to the exterior and interior furnishings of a building than we do to the hidden parts upon which the others depend. Biblical church government requires a biblical foundation, and a multiplicity of ministry is a vital component of that foundation.

Chapter Four

MULTIPLICITY OF MINISTRY WITHIN THE LOCAL CHURCH

A multiplicity of ministry rather than a singularity of ministry is the scriptural pattern of church government. *Multiplicity of ministry* means a plurality of ministry—more than one. God's ministry toward man has always been multifaceted. Whether through the elders of Israel, the council at Jerusalem in Acts chapter 15, or in His provision for fivefold ministry offices in the Church, God's government has always involved more than a single individual.

New Things

Remember ye not the former things, neither consider the things of old. Behold, I will do a new thing; now it shall spring forth; shall ye not know it? I will even make a way in the wilderness, and rivers in the desert (Isaiah 43:18-19).

God has always blessed the obedience of His commands, and for His blessing to continue, we must obey what He is saying to do now. He is revealing more and more of His plan, and He has times and seasons for His will to be accomplished. God has given us an enormously wonderful message that has been caught in the spirit of spiritual evolution and brought back to us in restoration.

And the voice spake unto him again the second time, What God hath cleansed, that call not thou common. This was done thrice: and the vessel was received up again into heaven. Now while Peter doubted in himself what this vision which he had seen should mean, behold, the men which were sent from Cornelius had made inquiry for Simon's house, and stood before the gate (Acts 10:15-17).

And when Peter was come up to Jerusalem, they that were of the circumcision contended with him, saying, Thou wentest in to men uncircumcised, and didst eat with them. But Peter rehearsed the matter from the beginning, and expounded it by order unto them, saying....Then remembered I the word of the Lord, how that He said, John indeed baptized with water; but ye shall be baptized with the Holy Ghost. Forasmuch then as God gave them the like gift as He did unto us, who believed on the Lord Jesus Christ; what was I, that I could withstand God? (Acts 11:2-4, 16-17)

And certain men which came down from Judaea taught the brethren, and said, Except ye be circumcised after the manner of Moses, ye cannot be saved (Acts 15:1).

Since the plan of God is continually unfolding (evolving), what worked and seemed to be acceptable yesterday may not be so today. In the above account in the Book of Acts, God's purpose had turned toward the Gentiles. God miraculously revealed this to Peter, and through Peter to the early Church. First the religious minds of that day had to accept that God desired to save the Gentiles. Then they had to embrace a new teaching—that the Gentiles did not require circumcision for salvation.

God was doing a new thing, but they had great difficulty in accepting it. Not only did it go against their tradition, it also went against clear statements of Scripture.

*And he that is eight days old shall be circumcised among you, every man child in your generations, he that is born in the house, or bought with money of any stranger, which is not of thy seed. He that is born in thy house, and he that is bought with thy money, must needs be circumcised: and My covenant shall be in your flesh for an **everlasting covenant**. And the uncircumcised man child whose flesh of his foreskin is not circumcised, that soul **shall be cut** off from his people; he hath broken My covenant* (Genesis 17:12-14, emphasis added).

Today, many in religious legalism cite Scripture to support their various contentions. This, of course, is nothing new. The dispute over circumcision in the early Church was the single most significant issue facing the young Church. Those who supported the necessity of circumcision pointed to Scriptures such as the above that clearly called circumcision an *"everlasting covenant"* for all generations and plainly stated that those who were not circumcised would be cut off from God's people.

We can see why theirs was such a powerful position. What they did not understand, however, was that God's purpose toward man is continually evolving; that only ministry properly ordered would be able to receive a proceeding Word from God. In stating the official position of the Church, James used the principle of spiritual evolution when quoting from Amos and decreeing that circumcision for Gentiles was not mandatory. God, in essence, was doing a new thing as indicated by the Scripture regarding the reestablishment of David's tabernacle.

God at one time decreed that animals be offered as sacrifice for sin. This was mandated and spoken of in many Scriptures. Yet today, we no longer offer animal sacrifice for sin. We have experienced a spiritual evolution. We know that Jesus was given as a sacrifice for the sins of the whole world and is the only sacrifice sufficient for sin.

Spiritual Evolution

"Spiritual evolution" (not to be confused with the theory of evolution) is the unfolding or gradually developing plan and purpose of God from time to time, and from one point to another. God did enormously marvelous things in the beginning, but these beginning works were not the extent of His approach or plan. His plan toward man is continually unfolding or evolving toward its ultimate conclusion.

The works of God are accelerating and changing, because God is constantly exceeding what He has done before. If God did something wonderful and abundant in the past, He can do something even more wonderful and abundantly above that in the future. God may have gone as far as you thought He could possible go today, but if you look around tomorrow, He will have gone even further. The apostle Paul taught of God's exceeding greatness toward us in the Book of Ephesians.

> That the God of our Lord Jesus Christ, the Father of glory, may give unto you the spirit of wisdom and revelation in the knowledge of Him: the eyes of your understanding being enlightened; that ye may know...what is the exceeding greatness of His power to us-ward who believe, according to the working of His mighty power (Ephesians 1:17-19).

In the beginning, God gave us a son by creation in Adam; then He gave Isaac, a son by promise in Abraham; and ultimately, a Son by the virgin birth in Jesus Christ, who gave us the redemption that Adam could not give. God's plan and program toward man is accelerating. Things that once were important, things that once were God, things God once blessed are not necessarily the things He is now doing or blessing. There is always an escalation of God's plan toward us.

Man strives to do his greatest deeds, but God continually exceeds His own greatness. God is always unfolding His plan though a greater revelation of who He is and how His Spirit operates. The plan for mankind through His first son, Adam, is brought to completion through His second Son, Jesus. The power of His law yields in its strength to the wonder of His grace.

God had to do away with the first (animal sacrifices for sin), that He might establish the second (the sacrifice of Jesus). If the law had been God's highest order, we would have missed grace. He does away with one thing to bring another order in. If God were not moving, if there were no spiritual evolution of things, there would be no grace because law would have been God's greatest invention, and He would have stayed with it forever.

> *To what purpose is the multitude of your sacrifices unto Me?* *saith the Lord: I am full of the burnt offerings of rams, and the fat of fed beasts; and I delight not in the blood of bullocks, or of lambs, or of he goats. When ye come to appear before Me,* **who hath required this at your hand,** *to tread My courts? Bring no more vain oblations; incense is an abomination unto Me; the new moons and sabbaths, the calling of assemblies, I cannot away with; it is iniquity, even the solemn meeting. Your new moons and your appointed feasts my soul hateth: they are a trouble unto Me; I am weary to bear them* (Isaiah 1:11-14, emphasis added).

God is continually moving, prodding His Church to come higher, to understand what it is that the Church is to be doing. God at one time commanded animal sacrifice, the offering of incense, and sacred assemblies at special times during the year. His purpose was to instruct and bring His people beyond their flesh into spiritual realms.

He not only gave them a plan, but a pattern. He is not interested in our sacrifice but in our change. This is why *"to obey is better than sacrifice, and to hearken than the fat of rams"*

(1 Sam. 15:22b). Obedience leads to righteousness, but sacrifice without obedience leads to self-righteousness.

In the Book of Isaiah, the Lord spoke to His people. His purpose was the manifestation of greater things. Although His desire was for increased relationship with His people, they were not drawing near unto Him. What was meant to bring relationship instead brought separation because of their disobedience. To demonstrate this, God would evolve His purpose toward man.

No longer would He delight in the very things He commanded them to do and would even ask of them, "Hey Israel, who asked you to do these things?" "Well, of course, You did, God, so why are You so displeased?" Why? Because the purpose of these ordinances was not to be found in the act itself, but rather in the ultimate purpose of bringing people higher and nearer unto Him.

In the beginning, God ordained a blood sacrifice for a man. In Egypt, He ordained a lamb for a family to spare the firstborn. That was not broad enough, so for the children of Israel in the wilderness, He instituted a lamb for a nation. Ultimately, He determined it would require a Lamb for the world. God gave the Lamb of God to take away the sins of the world.

Therefore if any man be in Christ, he is a new creature: old things are passed away; behold, all things are become new (2 Corinthians 5:17).

God is always removing the old to establish the new. We need to become vessels that contain the new. The new things of God cannot be put into old wineskins. This transformation requires a willingness to let go of the old so that we can move on with God into new places. He is taking His people from law to grace and from a family to a nation, from association to relationship, and from their need to His desire.

God Is Always Moving

God is always moving. In the beginning, the Spirit of the Lord moved on the waters. At the end of the Book of Revelation are the words, *"Come, Lord Jesus."* And in between these two events, *"...as many as are led by the Spirit of God they are the sons of God"* (Rom. 8:14). There is a constant movement and leading of His Spirit.

> *Hear my prayer, O Lord, and give ear unto my cry; hold not Thy peace at my tears: for I am a stranger with Thee, and a sojourner, as all my fathers were* (Psalm 39:12).

As with natural Israel, we are a holy nation of sojourners traveling from a temporary land of wandering to a permanent land of promise, called forth by the Spirit to hear and follow His voice wherever He would lead. As He did with David and all the fathers, the Lord has also charted a course for us to follow, leading to the completion of His will. God's people will never find perfect rest until they are reunited in fullness with their God.

"Let us labour therefore to enter into that rest" (Heb. 4:11a). If we labor for anything, it should be to enter into the rest of God—not just rest in the sense of repose, but into the rest (the remainder) of God. God is evolving His purpose, intention, and provision toward us. The remainder of what God has for us comes through a spiritual evolution. We learn to move with God. It is a learned art. *"In Him we live, and move, and have our being"* (Acts 17:28a). It is progressive.

Everyone who chooses to stand still in God actually slides back. He may think he is standing firm in what God has said He is, but because God is doing a new thing, the breach between where that person stands and where God actually is moving becomes wider and wider.

God's character never changes; the nature of His truth remains the same. It is a *constant*. However, His manner of working out His plan is a *variable*. The attitude of God can never be stationary but constantly moving in His progressive will. God is always doing another thing. To understand this, we need to understand what things in God are constant and what things are variables.

The Doctrine of Constants and Variables

The two categories of God's working toward us are found in an understanding of constants and variables. Constants are those truths in God that never change, similar to the North Star that remains in the same place. Using this star, ships can navigate because it appears to never move.. It is constant and can be relied upon to always stay the same. Jesus Christ is the Son of God, redemption is by His blood, Jesus Christ was born of a virgin, the mercy of God endures forever, and God's truth endures to all generations. These are constants that never change.

On the other hand, in our presentation of the gospel, there are a multitude of things incorporated—some of which are truths God has given for a particular time but which do not remain constant for eternity. These are called variables because they can and sometimes do change. The variables support the constants.

For example, we need church services in order to gather together. The time or place for services could change, but the eternal truths preached there cannot be altered. An example of a variable is the moon that is not always in the same place but changes its position relative to the earth's horizon.

Tradition as It Relates to Constants and Variables

For laying aside the commandment of God, ye hold the tradition of men, as the washing of pots and cups: and many other such like things ye do. And He said unto them, Full well ye reject the commandment of God, that ye may keep your own tradition (Mark 7:8-9).

Jesus knew that truth bound by tradition hinders the continued understanding of the Word. Eventually, it will put people in a position where the tradition itself will compete with the growth and expanding comprehension of His Word. In God, there are some truths that move as His plan for mankind unfolds. The truth remains the same, but how it is applied in the light of greater understanding may change. If our application fails to change as our understanding grows, we will turn God's truth into the traditions of men.

And He came to Nazareth, where He had been brought up: and, as His custom was, He went into the synagogue on the sabbath day, and stood up for to read (Luke 4:16).

And the multitude of them that believed were of one heart and of one soul: neither said any of them that ought of the things which he possessed was his own; but they had all things common (Acts 4:32).

And Paul after this tarried there yet a good while, and then took his leave of the brethren, and sailed thence into Syria, and with him Priscilla and Aquila; having shorn his head in Cenchrea: for he had a vow (Acts 18:18).

It was the custom of Jesus to teach in the synagogue on the sabbath; the Christians at Jerusalem held all possessions in common; the apostle Paul made a vow and shaved his head—these were variables and not constants. They were applicable for these individuals at that particular time, but not mandatory for all believers at all times.

If a church used the above patterns and required teaching at every church service or demanded that Christians practice communal living or insisted that all ministry must take a vow at certain times and shave their heads, these practices would be viewed as highly legalistic. Yet this is exactly what many have done. But because they have practiced their variables for so long, they have turned them into constants, and do not recognize them for what they are.

The Lord may lead some Christians into the synagogue or the church world to preach. He may give a directive and demonstrate spiritual truths with natural manifestation (such as to the Jerusalem Church regarding possessions). But to command that these things be continually observed would be making variables into constants that all must heed.

The result is a legalistic application of the Christian life. Not only have many made constants out of variables, but they have made constants out of a misapplication of Scripture. The result of both is legalistic tradition.

Tradition is a result of confusing variables and constants, such as esteeming the means of conveying truth, with the same importance as truth itself. The Pharisees held to all manner of self-imposed laws concerning what to touch and not touch, what to eat and how far to walk. They made constants out of variables. They also made variables out of constants by failing to implement the spirit behind the law as Jesus said, you *"have omitted the weightier matters of the law, judgment, mercy, and faith"* (Mt. 23:23b).

Variables can become tradition when something set in place by the elders is practiced over a long period of time without the understanding of why it was implemented in the first place. These traditions, which are the work of our hands, compete with God's Word and become idols. Consequently, when God seeks to deal with us, these idols are barricading the way. As the prophet of God said to Israel, "Thy calf, O Samaria, hath cast thee off" (Hosea 8:5a).

Forasmuch as ye know that ye were not redeemed with corruptible things, as silver and gold, from your vain conversation received by tradition from your fathers (1 Peter 1:18).

66

I am verily a man, which am a Jew...and was zealous toward God, as ye all are this day. And I persecuted this way unto the death, binding and delivering into prisons both men and women (Acts 22:3-4).

The apostle Paul was a man zealous toward God, yet tradition turned his desire to walk in the truth of God into a ministry that was actually contrary to and in opposition with God. His persecution of the early Church was with the best motives and intentions. He was zealous for the traditions of the fathers.

In his mind, he was not opposing God, but rather, he was defending the faith. Was Paul sincere in walking according to the Word? Yes...but he was sincerely wrong. He knew the Scripture, but he did not know the true heart of the God of Scripture. Paul was promoting his own understanding of Scripture as the truth and the will of God, but was actually in direct opposition to that will. He had His constants and variables all mixed up.

Many people today establish constants by misapplying Scripture. Through misapplication, some command conformity to a certain mode of dress, a particular day of the week for worship, the silence of women in church, and even snake handling. Are bans on musical instruments in church, certain mandates on apparel, no use of electricity, and thousands of other beliefs held by various Christians considered variables of God, constants of God, or traditions of men made into constants?

Traditions of men can turn our fervency to do God's will into a devotion for the completion of our own will. They sap our spiritual strength, peace, and love, and make our Christianity a burden we must perform rather than a joy we are eager to live. They war with the ability of the Spirit to lead us higher. Traditions of men always move us to do a work for God while love always motivates us to do the work of God.

Men's traditions cause blindness toward the increased revelation of the Word. Since most religious traditions have some basis in Scripture, it is very difficult for those bound by tradition to distinguish between that which is tradition and that which is truth. The confusion over what are variables and what are constants have kept many in bondage to fear and traditions of men.

Those following after the traditions of their fathers tend to consider their traditions as holy unto the Lord; but how can anything be holy if the heart is not wholly in what is done? Tradition considers the act itself as holy but does not consider man's intention for doing it. If the heart is not in what is done, man has separated from being one with God in purpose and has made a variable a constant.

I delight to do Thy will, O my God: yea, Thy law is within my heart (Psalm 40:8).

For My yoke is easy, and My burden is light (Matthew 11:30).

If in your Christian service your yoke is not easy and the burden light, you are not yoked to Jesus, but to variables masquerading as constants.

The Relationship of Truth With Variables and Constants

A consideration of variables and constants and an increased understanding of what truth is can help free us from the bondage of traditions of men. Truth is not a destination, rather it is a highway. Truth that becomes a destination will eventually be made into a tradition. Truth that is a highway gives direction and leads to higher places in Christ. Truth is the road along which we pass on our way to the finished work of Christ.

Truth is not the accumulation of factual knowledge. Factual knowledge is true, but it is not of itself the truth. People can and do believe all kinds of true things without having the truth. Most in Christianity believe the Bible is the Word of God, that Jesus died for the sin of man, that God loves the world, etc. All these things are true, but they do not necessarily give the truth to those who believe them.

Jesus saith unto him, I am the way, **the truth,** *and the life* (John 14:6a, emphasis added).

Truth is a highway; it is also a way of thinking; and in its highest understanding, it is a person, Jesus Christ. Although we can believe true things, we will never have *the truth* until we know the one who is *the Truth.* Truth is not an end but the continuing revelation of God. All things that reveal God are true. All things that are meant to obscure or misrepresent Him are not of truth.

It is not truth but *the Truth* that brings liberty to our life: *"And ye shall know the truth, and the truth shall make you free"* (Jn. 8:32). Without Jesus, whatever truth we possess, we possess in darkness only. Traditions of men, because they war with the increased revelation of the truth—Jesus, can turn the light of Jesus into darkness.

If therefore the light that is in thee be darkness, how great is that darkness! (Matthew 6:23b)

If the truth we possess is bound by tradition, then it becomes partial truth, which is the worst kind of lie. The purpose of the truth is the greater and greater manifestation of Jesus Christ.

An instructor of the foolish, a teacher of babes, which hast the form of knowledge and of the truth in the law (Romans 2:20).

The apostle Paul makes a case that tradition is a "form of truth." This is why it is so difficult for many to practice spiritual discernment, because circumstances can look so much like the real thing but are really only a natural form. Tradition blocks our growing in the knowledge of Him. Those bound by religious tradition often use Scripture to support their contention that they are not following tradition, but the Word.

Ever learning, and never able to come to the knowledge of the truth (2 Timothy 3:7).

But speaking the truth in love, may grow up into Him in all things, which is the head, even Christ (Ephesians 4:15).

Truth will always manifest itself in love. If what is being spoken or ministered is not done in love, it is not truth. Many will quote Scripture (all Scripture is true), but if the Scripture spoken is not spoken in love, it is not of truth.

And certain men which came down from Judaea taught the brethren, and said, Except ye be circumcised after the manner of Moses, ye cannot be saved (Acts 15:1).

The whole event surrounding the issue of circumcision in the early Church provides a window to not only understanding constants and variables but also church government. The latter will be dealt with in a subsequent chapter. Those of the circumcision held that salvation required one to be circumcised, and they had good Scripture to support their belief, such as the following verses:

He that is born in thy house, and he that is bought with thy money, must needs be circumcised: and My covenant shall be in your flesh for an everlasting covenant. And the uncircumcised man child whose flesh of his foreskin is not circumcised, that soul shall be cut off from his people; he hath broken My covenant (Genesis 17:13-14).

This Scripture clearly states that circumcision is necessary for an everlasting covenant. However, those of the circumcision did not realize or were blinded by tradition causing them to make a variable into a constant. The Scriptures presuming to support their position seemed so sound and clear that anyone should be able to see it. It was so apparent to them, that not to require circumcision was wholly contrary to the teachings of Scripture.

In actuality, the truth of covenant had not changed, but God's approach had. James, citing Amos chapter 9, demonstrated that there was a progression in God's plan toward man and that the Gentiles did not require circumcision for salvation. Still, tradition held many from seeing the progressive Word of God. So strong was this tradition that Paul was to fight with this spirit during his entire ministry. Unfortunately, those who continued to hold this doctrine could not see past their tradition. The truth they had, had become a destination rather than a highway.

When variables are changed into constants or constants into variables, false doctrines are created. When variables are turned into constants, we create tradition. When constants are turned into variables, we create heresy. If someone says, for example, that Jesus is not God, he has just turned a constant into a variable creating heresy. Both heresy and tradition of men hinder the revelation of the truth.

Let us consider the life of Mary. God chose Mary to fulfill His purpose for a set time. If Joseph would have put her away, he would have thwarted the plan and purpose of God. However, the facts are: She was not forever a virgin (the Bible names her children); she was not divine or one to be worshiped; she did not ascend into Heaven to make intercession for us. That is the work of Jesus Christ alone, and He is the One to be worshiped.

Jesus is the constant. Mary was the variable. *"Blessed art thou among women"* (Lk. 1:28b). God had other possibilities. A concept that God gives is important enough that it should not be thrown away but rather used in its time. Tradition gets the variables and constants mixed up making the concept the purpose. The purpose was not Mary. The purpose was Jesus.

When Jacob awoke after he saw the ladder into Heaven, he erected a pillar to mark the spot where he had encountered God. He called it Bethel (house of God). As important as this place was to Jacob, it did not hold an unchangeable place in his heart. It did not become an idol to him.

It was a place that became precious to Jacob when he was fleeing from his brother Esau, but because the God of the place was greater than the place itself, Jacob's understanding and experience was able to grow. Jacob later renamed this place El Bethel (God of the house). He had progressed from knowing where God was to knowing who God is. That is a spiritual evolution that many never go through.

We may recognize that God is or has been in our church, our denomination, or among us, and still not really know Him in His present workings. Things that God once said to do can become an idol to us that we vow never to let go of, and therefore, we miss the current Word of God. For example, a grove, (a group of trees), was planted to preserve the place where an altar once stood, at which God at one time had powerfully met with someone. God eventually condemned the groves because people began to worship the place where God once was instead of continuing to seek His ongoing purpose that would have shown them new and greater things.

When the generations who followed saw the groves, they counted them as holy places; and instead of worshiping God, who once answered by fire upon an altar, they set in those places idols and worshiped the works of their own hands. It is a reasonable question for any minister to ask himself, whether or not the work he is doing is the work of his own hands. Is it really a God-ordained work or a work ordained by man for God? In the modern church, when God answers by fire at one time in one way, we tend to cling to that forever, forgetting that God can exceed His own greatness and wants to do something else. He wants to move on.

The Fear of Change in the Church

Change is not easy; however, without change, the Church becomes stale as a result of being "stuck in a rut" for years. Many times, people strive to hold onto positions, titles, and traditions; but these keep them locked into what God once initiated and blessed. They hinder them from following after God when His plan escalates and He moves on to greater things. Consequently, the leadership becomes bound with fear that the people will rebel against change.

Ministry must be freed from the expectation of the people. A multiplicity of ministry cuts through traditions that have led to an improper understanding of ministry. When a multiplicity is instituted, it frees both saint and clergy to walk in proper ministry. We need to ask if the way we understand and implement ministry within the local church is done according to an evolution of a biblical pattern from God or as a result of tradition handed down by men.

Chapter Five

—•••••—

THE ALIGNMENT
OF CHURCH GOVERNMENT

Government is the process by which order is established
and maintained within the church. All churches operate via
some form of government. These governmental structures set
forth an operation of the church as to its finances, authority,
beliefs, and duties. The necessity of allowing for human
involvement in church organization while at the same time
providing liberty of the Spirit to rule, has always been a
dilemma to those seeking to provide a setting in which the
Spirit has supremacy. The establishment of biblical government through the multiplicity of ministry is the only way in
which the Spirit is truly free to rule His Church.

Consequences of Traditional Church Government

The doctrine of the Nicolaitans was the work of the laity
or people. In this system, the laity assumed authority over the
ministry. God hated it because the people ruled by voting for
what they wanted, thus removing God's guidance and violating
His order. In this case, people held the leadership in bondage
by their resistance to change. A corollary to the doctrine of the
Nicolaitans was the rule of the clergy over the people. In any
case, whether the people are in charge or the clergy is lording
over the people, God is not allowed to rule in His Church.
Either case elevates man over God.

A hireling can be a church leader or a church staff member filling the position simply to receive wages and not for the reason of ministering God's truth to the people; but nowhere in the Bible do you find a church operated by such a leader or staff.

We either have proper ministry, or we have a mess. Hired preachers do not necessarily love sheep. As stated before, a hireling is one who holds a position motivated by compensation. A true shepherd is one who holds a position motivated by relationship.

> *But he that is an hireling, and not the shepherd, whose own the sheep are not, seeth the wolf coming, and leaveth the sheep, and fleeth: and the wolf catcheth them, and scattereth the sheep. The hireling fleeth, because he is an hireling, and careth not for the sheep* (John 10:12-13).

Those who depend on performance to support their burden for the work of God will be the first to resist change, because if God does a new thing, they will lose their position or have their job greatly altered. When God escalates a plan, many times initial changes start at the foundation level before working their way up. Some people become offended and bitter if these changes cause them to be removed from an office or position that they have held for a long time.

Offense and bitterness are a result of carnal reasoning and a lack of spiritual perception. True faith acknowledges God and trusts in His ability to make out of us all that He has destined. If we are worried about keeping a position or frustrated by not acquiring the place of ministry we desire, we may be thinking carnally instead of motivated by a desire for God's will to manifest.

If people walk in the Spirit, the works of the flesh will not be manifested. God does not enlarge many churches because doing so would add prosperity to the prostitution of religion.

76

Those people added would be placed in the same bondage by which the church is bound. Men have built large churches, but size does not mean that it is God's design.

God has a current plan and purpose. If we do not align ourselves with it, God will move on to those who will, and leave us powerless and guilty before Him. The ministry should endeavor to bring the Church to a high spiritual level and should pray for courage and wisdom, trying not to change everything at one time.

In the multitude of counselors there is safety (Proverbs 11:14b).

Decisions concerning change should not be made alone but with counsel from peer brethren. God provides a presbytery of peer ministry for support, counsel, and protection to the set ministry. Ministry fathers and peer ministry provide security and strength for the set minister as well as the people. Peer ministry, as the name implies, are trusted ministry with an equal or greater rule than the set minister of the church. They are taken from outside the local church and are given authority to speak to the set minister regarding situations of a personal or church nature.

We can facilitate God's adding to the Church by our proper alignment with His order for church government and implementing a network to care for new believers. Many of our present church governments have been borrowed from years and years of episcopal systems and not from the Bible. By "episcopal," we are referring to the method of organization and not to the denomination that bears the same name.

Doing Right Things in the Wrong Way

Religious order rather than Kingdom order often starts with a proper concept that evolves into men's traditions contrary to the purpose of God. After a while the propagation of the concept becomes more important than the purpose for which it was founded (changing variables to constants). This causes many in Christianity to become destined to die in a religious system without ever experiencing the Kingdom. God wants to bring into being the biblical order of multiplicity of ministry to replace that of a solitary minister.

The genuine harvest can be reaped after the systems of men and hirelings are put aside and God's order of leadership is put in place. David had to remove the ark from the cart and have it carried by the priests for God's will to be done. To the religious mind, it seemed good to put the ark of God on a new cart. God, however, would not submit to man's wisdom. He would be carried only upon the shoulders (proper government) of those ordered for the task.

In another instance, God told Moses to set a serpent of brass on a pole so the people could see it and live. It was very important and was referred to in the New Testament as well:

"And as Moses lifted up the serpent in the wilderness, even so must the Son of man be lifted up" (John 3:14).

And Moses made a serpent of brass, and put it upon a pole, and it came to pass, that if a serpent had bitten any man, when he beheld the serpent of brass, he lived (Numbers 21:9).

The people of Israel were murmuring against God and Moses. They were discouraged about the journey and loathed the manna that God had provided. And indeed, they were intent on letting Moses know how they felt. The words of the serpent that beguiled Eve had infected this people as well. In His mercy, God answered the people's cry through His minister, Moses. The serpent that had been raised up in their minds was now a brass serpent nailed on a pole. God ministered their healing through His true minister, Moses.

All the people could see the source of their judgment, and those who could really see (those who could understand) were delivered. However, this brass serpent eventually became an idol in the house of God. What was once God's deliverance for the people had become an idol worshiped by the people.

Did God command its construction? Yes. Was it for His purpose? Yes. Did it become an idol? Yes. Can something commanded by God for His purpose become an idol? Yes, if the object is worshiped instead of the Source of its power. Are there concepts that ministry clings to for its life that are no longer in God's purpose, but idolatry? Yes.

Hezekiah found the people offering incense to the brazen snake in the temple. Even though God had ordained the serpent in the wilderness to take away death, Hezekiah said that now it was nothing but a piece of brass. He destroyed it and the groves. This story reveals that God is continually progressing. We embrace His eternal truths, yet we must allow Him freedom to move in a new way.

Often, it is more convenient and less unsettling to build around us a stagnant God. Stagnant waters, however, have no force or movement, but allow for the formation of polluted ponds. God is always moving, and we must learn to move with Him. Only new wineskins are able to carry and dispense living water.

The Need for New Wineskins

The Church needs the government of God as a new wineskin to hold the truth of God, the love of God, the harvest of God, the purpose of God, and the manifestation of God. As the vascular system of blood that is the life of a body is held by tissue and muscle and protected by skin, so the Church needs biblical government. Truth, the gospel, and redemption are the purpose of the Church, but there has to be structure to keep it all together. It is church government that not only holds it together but also allows for the expansion of gospel truth.

Change Is Essential

Change is the oft-used device of God to bring sanctification to the Church. Since God is always moving, we need to be willing and flexible to accept change. What we have in God may be good, but our change into His nature can give us an increased measure of His nature.

Even though it is at times painful, God is bringing the Church into proper alignment out of men's traditions and into His perfection. Desire to change is conceived in a person's spirit, and it grows in the heart; but the birthing of it is difficult. It is similar to a mother going through a transitional phase before giving birth to a child. Although we have God's message, we continue to use men's methods of carrying it. We will remain out of order unless we are willing to change.

> *And they said one to another, Let us make a captain, and let us return into Egypt* (Numbers 14:4).

The essence of repentance is change. Turning from our methods of church government to God's methods requires a willingness to not only obey but to change. Some who seek to obey never change because their heart is not sold out to the new thing God is doing. They talk the talk, but they don't walk the walk. Like Israel, they may grudgingly leave their old habitations, but they never really change. They long for a return to that *from which God has provided deliverance and continually are at variance with the leadership God has placed over them.*

> *But we all, with open face beholding as in a glass the glory of the Lord, are changed into the same image from glory to glory, even as by the Spirit of the Lord* (2 Corinthians 3:18).

We are to go from glory to glory, from victory to victory, from faith to faith. God sees all things from the end to the beginning. Knowing the fullness of His plan, He allows things to happen to fulfill that plan. The Lord told Jeremiah, *"to root out, and to pull down, and to destroy, and to throw down, to build, and to plant"* (Jer. 1:10b).

That which is wrong must be changed, but it is useless to move from one carnal method to another. Biblical, foundational, and constitutional change needs to be made, so we can move in the purpose of God. When we change, we need to go from victory to victory, not from mess to mess; from faith to faith, not from tragedy to tragedy; from glory to glory, not from discouragement to discouragement.

God's Pattern Versus Man's Pattern

See, saith He, that thou make all things according to the pattern shown to thee in the mount (Hebrews 8:5b).

This Scripture refers to church government that is demonstrated in the priesthood and order of the tabernacle of Moses. Presently, the Church has been following its own pattern rather than God's pattern, and it has assumed that its good intentions can take the place of God's established order. But our good intentions and the good works of our own hands are no substitute for learning to follow the movement of God. In fact, to do His will and to truly obey, we need to be able to understand and follow the moving of God.

Although Abraham produced a son, Ishmael, by the bondwoman, it was not God's ordained plan. Abraham did not clearly understand how God planned to do what He had promised, and it may have occurred to him that some action on his part, not specifically decreed by God, was required to bring the promise to pass. When God gives ministry a promise, it often seeks to help God out, especially if the promise is some time in coming.

81

Hope sees into our future, but faith allows us to walk it out step by step. Faith requires understanding and a character that allows us to see beyond current circumstance. Our fears and impatience will war against our faith, and in trying to help God beyond our understanding, we often prolong our process.

Rather than devising a plan of our imagination, we should seek *His* pattern. God always follows His pattern for our ministries. We may pout and weep, but God is not moved. He will not conform to our ministry imaginations but allows time and process to turn us toward His pattern. His will and not ours will be done. We may establish a ministry order birthed in our imaginations and good intentions, but it is the Lord's pattern of multiplicity of ministry that will eventually rule in His Church.

God's order ultimately brought Isaac into being. Abraham's plan did not become a replacement for God's willed plan. We either do things the Lord's way, or we endure struggle until we alter our way to meet His. If we do not do it the Lord's way, sometimes the things birthed in our ignorance, frustration, or self-will become oppositions to the birthing and nurturing of that given from God.

It requires a real and painful rending to put away our own will, which seeks to put into bondage what was birthed by God. We can get to the place where we are uncertain exactly what God has said. Our human understanding about how to help God give us the promises He has spoken to us, often is the source of our greatest frustrations.

David's first attempt to return the ark to Jerusalem met with disaster. David and the people had good intentions, but their good intentions were no substitute for God's order. It was right to bring the ark back, but the method of transportation was wrong. In the same manner, we have a good message, but bad transportation. We often try to carry the divine in a cart made out of our human understanding and good intentions.

If we could ever match our methods with the message, we could win the world. One of the elders died as he touched the ark to steady it. He desired to do a good and seemingly right thing. His intentions were honorable, but his understanding and conduct were not in God's order.

So also, when our methods are out of order, good people may be destroyed by participating in the man-made method that has been created by the hands of ministry; consequently, the great move of God is "left in Obededom's house." *Obededom* means "servant of Edom." God would rather remain in an earthly system until proper order is reestablished than be brought back to His proper place according to man's order.

Proper order predicates all that we do because it speaks of the divine influence in our lives. What we do in our ministries should always be according to divine order—meaning, it is God's plan of action and not how we think it should be done. God's thoughts are higher than our thoughts, and our ways are not His. If we want our ministry to prosper, then we better align ourselves to His thoughts.

Insight From the Construction of God's House

Obededom's home was blessed because the ark was in his house, even though its place should have been resting in Jerusalem. Eventually, David had the ark moved on the shoulders of the priests as God commanded. The cart might have appeared to be a better method, but God moves on animate objects that have a destiny—not on inanimate objects that have only purpose.

God moves on men, not on systems. Systems have no heart or conscience and can destroy ministries that are precious. With all our bylaws, constitutions, and manipulations, we finally have to realize the Church is not a business. It affects people's lives. It is alive, and no system or entity can take the place of living people who have learned how to love and know how to be obedient to God. Not only those in the world, but those in church as well are longing to go beyond the staleness of religious systems and be touched by the love of God and the life of the called-out saints who are the real Church.

So the house of the Lord was perfected (2 Chronicles 8:16; see also 8:14).

While workmen were constructing the physical building, Solomon diligently studied the order that God had given his father, David, concerning ministry in the temple. Solomon studied the order of his father. Father/son order is an indispensable avenue for developing and maintaining the order of God.

In like manner, we need to seek God's order for ministry in the house. It is often difficult to change our methods because we have too much at stake in our religious system. But we must have grace to be willing to make major changes because churches, congregations, and positions can be lost. To do the work of God we must usually undo the work of our own hands.

Many times it is hard to consider: Did God call me to this place? Am I doing what I was called to do? Where am I in the fivefold ministry? Am I in proper alignment in the Kingdom of God? Change can be difficult and tradition dies screaming, yet it brings great relief to find what we are and who we are supposed to become. The pain of change brings the joy and security of knowing that we will complete the ministry entrusted into our care.

Some know only the security of bondage to the familiar. Most of the Israelites, at one time, sought the security of bondage in Egypt over the promise of God in a new land. There is a much greater, howbeit less welcome, security in change that many never experience. Learning to live in the change of God is the only method that gives us the assurance of knowing and completing our divine destiny.

New Testament Examples of Multiplicity of Ministry

The New Testament establishes an order of multiplicity of ministry in the Church, and we need to follow this New Testament pattern. Following the biblical pattern will require significant changes in the order of most local churches. For example, in most churches, provision is made for only a pastor or a limited staff; therefore, the other areas of fivefold ministry are not provided for financially. How the organization of the local church is viewed will have to be greatly adjusted in order to bring forth a multiplicity of ministry.

In the Antioch church, there were teachers and prophets, not just the single pastor ministry. This church had a multiplicity of ministry—a many-functioned ministry that sent out ministry, implemented the directives of the Holy Spirit, taught, preached, prophesied, and gave oversight to the entire local body. Even the apostle Paul was submitted to its leadership.

> *Then tidings of these things came unto the ears of the church which was in Jerusalem: and they sent forth Barnabas, that he should go as far as Antioch. And when he had found him, he brought him unto Antioch. And it came to pass, that a whole year they assembled themselves with the church, and taught much people. And the disciples were called Christians first in Antioch* (Acts 11:26b; see also 11:22).

> *Now there were in the church that was at Antioch certain prophets and teachers; as Barnabas, and Simeon that was called Niger, and Lucius of Cyrene, and Manaen, which had been brought up with Herod the tetrarch, and Saul* (Acts 13:1).

> *Then pleased it the apostles and elders, with the whole church, to send chosen men of their own company to Antioch*

85

with Paul and Barnabas; namely, Judas surnamed Barsabas, and Silas, chief men among the brethren (Acts 15:22).

And when he had landed at Caesarea, and gone up, and saluted the church, he went down to Antioch (Acts 18:22).

Even the so-called "great" apostle Paul was not a freelance minister. He, as all true ministries, fell under the authority of God's government. Paul was held accountable. The church at Antioch sent him out, and it was to them he reported upon his return. Antioch was not under a church system, but under a multiplicity of ministry. Antioch was a church that was properly taught and one that was in order. It was at Antioch that they were first called Christians, because it was here that they first learned the disciplines of Christ that required proper church government. In the Antioch church, we find multiplicity of ministry operating through a plurality of ministry.

Nowhere in the New Testament is someone called "the pastor" of a church with a one-man leadership role. Plurality of eldership is the New Testament plan. They ordained elders (plural), in every church (city) (see Acts 14:23). God always sets a man (set ministry) in leadership who raises elders into their place of oversight.

Ministry Sons—a Requirement for Multiplicity of Ministry

If we do not raise up sons in the gospel, the principle of the multiplicity of ministry will be lacking. Those forming the multiplicity of ministry in a local church must have more than a denominational connection with each other. If multiplicity is a many-faceted ministry, then the many facets must derive their connection through relationship and not just position. In fact, proper ministry must be the outgrowth of true relationship.

There must be birthed in us the willingness to teach and impart from the Spirit into the lives of prospective elders. An eldership with different visions gathered from various places probably will not unite under a single vision and function properly because it is usually not birthed in relationship but in gifting or in need. A common vision is essential in not only furthering the work but in establishing unity of the Body.

As a result of competition with other churches, sometimes people with talent are invited to join the ministry of another church—even if they lack the vision of that ministry. This is done because of lust for Kingdom preeminence and lack of Kingdom consciousness. The leadership is not so much concerned for the ministry to the saints as much as they jealously desire to compete with all other churches on the "cutting edge." This results in disunity and creates a sibling rivalry in the staff. It wars against relationship, so at best, it can only bring a forced unity within the church.

A minister can have a large church, a financially prosperous ministry, and a work of note throughout the church community without ever following a multiplicity of ministry. If these aspirations become the goal or vision of a ministry, they can be achieved without the establishment of a biblical government. To find and complete the vision of God, however, and to establish a work through subsequent generations, a church must have a multiplicity of ministry.

The local church should be a place where prospective ministries can be fathered and the vision of the house imparted to them, so they can walk in harmony with the local ministry. Every church should be a Bible school. When people are trained by another ministry, they receive another vision. A person who can be put in a place of trust and love is one whose heart is molded together with the leadership, as was Elisha with Elijah. Elisha was tested, but he left everything to follow Elijah. He said, "Wherever you are going, I am going" (see 2 Kings 2). When Elijah was taken up, Elisha said, *"My father, my father"* (2 Kings 2:12).

We need people who are with us in spirit, and not just those we choose because we feel they are gifted or have demonstrated a desire to be in ministry. People's "roots" need to be checked to see if they are in rebellion or if they just want a place to exercise their own ideas or ideologies. Ministry that comes from immature leaders such as these confuse the flock and potentially leach from the church spirituality.

Many times after being trained and raised up into the ministry of a church, a minister will say that God has called him to have his own church. Yet God has not called him unless he has a father who has called him out. If a true father has not said, "You are my son," the minister has no right to go forth in ministry.

> *...Elijah said...if thou see me when I am taken from thee* [which in the original language means, "if you see eye to eye with me when I leave"], *it shall be so unto thee* [you will receive a double portion of my spirit]; *but if not, it shall not be so* (2 Kings 2:9-10).

Each church must have a singleness of vision. We have so much trouble because everyone has his own vision. This is why there is often so much di-vision (two visions), in the local church. Can we even remotely believe that the Holy Spirit is ruling in a church when the mess and disorder in so much of the Church is evident even to the world?

The Call of Ministry

So the last shall be first, and the first last: for many be called, but few chosen (Matthew 20:16).

For many are called, but few are chosen (Matthew 22:14).

These shall make war with the Lamb, and the Lamb shall overcome them: for He is Lord of lords, and King of kings: and they that are with Him are called, and chosen, and faithful (Revelation 17:14).

88

The phrase, "many are called, but few are chosen," is used in the Gospel of Matthew in connection with servants desiring position and reward. Many are called into service, but few are found able to enter into greater service. Those with the Lamb, who are able to come over to higher places of responsibility, have been called, chosen, and faithful. As we shall see, it is God who does the calling; proper church government does the choosing; and the minister who is called must prove himself faithful.

> But seek ye first the kingdom of God, and His righteousness; and all these things shall be added unto you (Matthew 6:33).

The righteousness or right-ness of the Kingdom of God are to be sought first. A Kingdom-minded person destroys gossip, rebellion, and opposition to leadership. He desires God's Kingdom, not his own kingdom, and loves God's work more than he loves his own position, title, or wages. Change is not a problem because nothing is more important to him than the Kingdom of God. If a person is not Kingdom-conscious, he gets offended and starts his own church—but there is no grace to cover the ministry of that work. A person who loves the work of God and seeks to walk in Kingdom order will never lack a ministry position. His or her life will become the source of their ministry.

> For the kingdom of God is not meat and drink; but righteousness, and peace, and joy in the Holy Ghost (Romans 14:17).

The Kingdom cannot be attained through position or by titles. It is not manifested by the size or prominence of our ministries. It is found in the progression of three things— righteousness, peace, and joy—these being obtained through the Holy Spirit. Righteousness must come first—God's ways of being and doing. We must first seek His way of being and

His way of doing things. There can be no right church order without a multiplicity of ministry.

Many are working where they are, not because God said to, but because it seemed a good thing to do or because they had trouble in the church where they formerly attended. Some were not brought to maturity because of disagreement with their pastor; consequently, they did not remain as a son in the house until the time to be sent forth by the Holy Ghost. Thus, the order of God is altered, and he or she operates outside the grace of God in frustration and futility, never learning the order of God. Ministry likewise must be in order or the operation of the Spirit can be limited.

One must be begotten by the teaching, instruction, vision, and purpose of a father with whom he can see eye to eye until the time comes to be sent forth or placed into ministry. Otherwise, a person operates outside the grace of God and has no right to minister. If people come with similar vision and burden, then you can very carefully watch growth in them until there is a father/son-type relationship established between you. The attitude becomes one of "What can I do for the Kingdom?" rather than "What can God do for me or through me?"

The Right of Ministry

Lay hands suddenly on no man, neither be partaker of other men's sins: keep thyself pure (1 Timothy 5:22).

We are coming out of a religious darkness. Reordering the Church will require a monumental effort. There will be a sifting of ideas and a challenge to our customary ways of thinking and acting. As we seek God's connections, we will be required to make adjustments. Some people we would never have thought about associating with in our religious attitudes may be the ones God is leading us to.

We must be patient and open to allow the Spirit to make our necessary connections. An immediate decision to accept someone before knowing his or her spirit could result in our becoming a part of their iniquity as well as their impurity becoming a part of us. We must be careful to put ourselves under authority of God's choosing and honest enough with ourselves not to let our flesh remove us from godly covering. There should be a constant search for other godly people of similar vision with the same precious faith.

The Lord says, *"I will build My church..."* (Mt. 16:18b). The father/son connection as well as a proper multiplicity of ministry is a spiritual order. In its final analysis, the right to ministry is about being open to the connections that the Spirit of God has ordained for each ministry and each local setting.

A presbytery is a group of people, including a ministry father, whom a leader or set man trusts to surround him and speak into his life. That presbytery should have the same vision that he has received from God. This can be a guard and protection for him as well as for those who surround him. There is security and strength for the church as well as for ministry in having a presbytery taken not from religious systems but from individuals outside the church who have like vision and spiritual rule. Preachers become self-appointed ministers when they decide for themselves that God wants them in ministry rather than through confirmation of the Spirit, the sanction of godly order, and the witness of a ministry father.

No man taketh this honour unto himself, but he that is called of God, as was Aaron (Hebrews 5:4).

The order of Aaron was predicated upon the spiritual principal that a priest must be the son of a priest—the priesthood was from father to son. Today, this does not speak of physical but spiritual parenthood. Most today take this honor unto themselves. They feel called and therefore have the right to establish their ministries without proper authority or vision.

In the gospels is listed the genealogy validating Jesus' right to ministry. Even with Jesus, His genealogy and the witness of His Father were necessary for ministry.

> *These sought their register among those that were reckoned by genealogy, but they were not found: therefore were they, as polluted, put from the priesthood* (Ezra 2:62).

The right to ministry in the Old Testament required substantiation of a priestly lineage. This is a type of the New Testament requirement to have a spiritual pedigree in order to enter ministry. True ministry must be received and passed on through relationship. When relationship is taken out of the equation, ministry becomes little more than the act of self-willed individuals who establish themselves in ministry by their own hand.

Ministry, in most places, is not from father to son, but from call of God to our attempts at self-fulfillment or worse, denomination bylaws to an approved licensee. In these cases, there is no establishment of a biblical multiplicity or authority. At one time, this was all most people in Christianity knew, but in this day, those desiring the Kingdom will not be able to attain it without ministry order.

Paul called Timothy, Titus, and others, sons. Jesus did not call Himself to preach but was called by Him, who said, *"Thou art My Son, today have I begotten Thee"* (Heb. 5:5b). His right to minister was that He was the Son of a Father. He could do nothing but what He saw the Father do. He did only that which was pleasing in the Father's sight, and He delighted to do the will of the Father. His purpose, identity, and ministry were so connected to the Father that He described their relationship as, "I and My Father are one" (Jn. 10:30).

There Are no Lone Rangers in Biblical Ministry

Often those in ministry see ministry as an independent work: It is "my ministry." On the contrary, all proper ministry is interdependent. No minister is an island. God has connected ministry together. This is in part the design of a multiplicity of ministry. The leader of a local church who fails to see that he is only part of the ministry of the church and that his ministry does not stand independent of the rest of the church, will continually be frustrated. He will most likely be turned inward, trying to build a work of his own efforts yet calling it the work of God.

> *And the Lord spake unto Moses, saying, Take the Levites instead of all the firstborn among the children of Israel, and the cattle of the Levites instead of their cattle; and the Levites shall be Mine: I am the Lord* (Numbers 3:44-45).

God didn't call Moses alone but the whole Levitical tribe. The whole local church Body should be a Body of ministry. Kingdom ministry is dependent upon it.

> *From thirty years old and upward even unto fifty years old, every one that came to do the service of the ministry, and the service of the burden in the tabernacle of the congregation* (Numbers 4:47).

There were certain tasks assigned according to maturity and family. Some offered sacrifice; some cared for the tabernacle; some supplied the needs of the tabernacle. It was not a one-man show.

> *And when the queen of Sheba had seen all Solomon's wisdom, and the house that he had built, and the meat of his table, and the sitting of his servants, and the attendance of his ministers, and their apparel, and his cupbearers, and his ascent by which he went up unto the house of the Lord; there was no more spirit in her* (1 Kings 10:4-5).

Solomon established a multiplicity of ministry according to that of his father David (father/son ministry order). When the Queen of Sheba came to see the glory of his kingdom, it was not his great wealth or his military might or the culture of the kingdom that impressed her. She had heard about these and had seen similar things in other places. What impressed the queen was the *order of the house*. Ministry in Solomon's court was in perfect order. This was the half that was not told to her. A local church and its ministry in proper order is a wonderful thing to behold.

> *For as we have many members in one body, and all members have not the same office: so we, being many, are one body in Christ, and every one members one of another. Having then gifts differing according to the grace that is given to us, whether prophecy, let us prophesy according to the proportion of faith; or ministry, let us wait on our ministering: or he that teacheth, on teaching; or he that exhorteth, on exhortation: he that giveth, let him do it with simplicity; he that ruleth, with diligence; he that showeth mercy, with cheerfulness. Let love be without dissimulation. Abhor that which is evil; cleave to that which is good* (Romans 12:4-9).

Ministry in the Body is multifaceted. The writers of the New Testament speak in many ways about the multiplicity of ministry in the Church, yet the emphasis, in the modern church, on singular or "elite" ministry has hindered the multifaceted and varied ministry of the Church.

> *For he was numbered with us, and had obtained **part of this ministry*** (Acts 1:17, emphasis added).

> *But we all, with open face beholding as in a glass the glory of the Lord, are changed into the same image from glory to glory, even as by the Spirit of the Lord. Therefore seeing **we have this ministry**, as we have received mercy, we faint not* (2 Corinthians 3:18–4:1, emphasis added).

*And all things are of God, who hath reconciled us to Him-self by Jesus Christ, and hath **given to us the ministry** of reconciliation* (2 Corinthians 5:18, emphasis added).

*And Barnabas and Saul returned from Jerusalem, when they had **fulfilled their ministry**, and took with them John, whose surname was Mark* (Acts 12:25, emphasis added).

Ye also helping together by prayer for us (2 Corinthians 1:11a).

The Bible never uses the phrase, "my ministry." It does speak of individual ministry as in Second Timothy 4:5, but never to the exclusion of other ministry. Timothy was part of Paul's ministry. Paul was part of the ministry of the Antioch church. In the Scriptures above, the apostles understood that each had a part in the same ministry. Paul uses phrases such as, *"we have this ministry,"* and makes note that the saints are par-takers in the work given him through their prayer. It was a cor-porate multiplicity of ministry.

Struggles Within Out-of-Order Ministries

Ministry that is without spiritual parental ties, and is not associated with a covering and fathership, has no biblical right to ministry. A minister cannot call himself to ministry, but must have a father who says, "You are my son." Fatherless min-istries become laws to themselves. They propagate tradition, perpetuating religion without proper government. In this way, many have come into the ministry, not having any other pat-tern to follow. Once God gives enlightenment, however, we ought to seek the revealed order.

The priesthood or ministry is surrounded by infirmity (their own problems as well as the problems of the people). They oftentimes find themselves in a position of operating outside the grace of God—where they do not offer more sacri-fice for themselves than for the people, or where they are appointed to a position or job in which God never called them, or where they have called themselves to preach.

They, therefore, and their ministries, are more likely to suffer from immorality, breakdowns, sickness, and tragedy. We take upon ourselves burdens and minister in areas for which God never gave us grace to accomplish. Paul said he was an apostle according to the grace given unto him. He could work only in that area because the grace of God given to him was already measured for apostleship and not for pastor or evangelist, etc.

If he had worked outside the area designated by God, he would have found himself outside of God's grace. Preacher burnout is often thought of as being the result of working too hard for God, but it is usually the consequence of working outside the plan, purpose, and structure of God. Doing the work we think God wants us to do or doing it in a way that frustrates His grace will cause exasperation and discouragement. If we learn to do the work of God rather than a work *for* God, it would eliminate much of the feeling of disappointment and defeat often experienced in ministry.

An out-of-order ministry places itself in a catch-22 situation. People may desire to do the will of God, but because of their improper biblical order, they find themselves incapable of doing so. How many in ministry could have been spared much heartache and pain had they only known about a multiplicity of ministry? How many who are no longer in active ministry are really called by God for this purpose, but because they labored within improper systems, they thought that the problem was with them? They really have heard God's call but did not have a structure through which it could be properly implemented.

For every high priest taken from among men is ordained for men in things pertaining to God, that he may offer both gifts and sacrifices for sins (Hebrews 5:1).

True ministers are God-directed people who come from men and whose purpose involves those they are taken from. They must be chosen from among men to serve for men and the Kingdom's sake and not for themselves. The Kingdom of God is more valuable than personal call, money, prestige, or ambition. Their desire must not be "my kingdom come" but "Thy Kingdom come."

True ministers must die to their own ways and seek God's cleansing and purging for themselves as well as for the people—realizing that those in ministry are surrounded and constantly encompassed by spiritual attack. There must be holiness and righteousness in leadership. The leader must offer sacrifices for the people and for himself. He is not exempt. He is not chosen because he is immaculate, and neither are the people. The Old Testament priest offered a sacrifice for himself and for the people.

Hebrews 5:2-3 continues speaking of the priest: *"Who can have compassion on the ignorant, and on them that are out of the way; for that he himself also is compassed with infirmity. And by reason hereof he ought, as for the people, so also for himself, to offer for sins."*

The one-man or board-operated pastoral system will never fulfill all that God has ordained. The harvest will be retained when the Church implements God's order.

Chapter Six

———•••••———

MINISTRY TITLES

The apostle Paul was not against tradition and even gave counsel to follow the traditions and instructions that were set for the Church. While there is a tradition of truth that is set and should be carried on, there is also the tradition of men.

Therefore, brethren, stand fast, and hold the traditions which ye have been taught, whether by word, or our epistle (2 Thessalonians 2:15).

The traditions of men are ideas with no particular consistency of truth or purpose, yet they are set forth and become a part of doctrinal belief. These are variable or changeable concepts that people attempt to make into constants and unalterable truths. The organization of much of modern Christianity is one such tradition that requires the scrutiny of all seeking godly order in the local church.

*Various Church Government Systems
as Opposed to the Multiplicity of Ministry*

Although there is little systematic instruction on church government in the New Testament writings, there is a distinct pattern of church organization. From the various types and inferences contained in Scripture, many forms of church government have come forth. Catholic, State, Presbyterian, Quaker, Oligarchic, to name a few, have evolved over time.

Indeed, one of the reasons thousands of Christian denominations have appeared over the years has to do with the issue of what the correct form of Christian church government is.

When speaking of types of church government, the vast majority fall within two broad categories that we can call *episcopal* and *congregational*. These terms should not be confused with denominations of the same names.

The word *episcopal* refers to local government by an individual, commonly called a pastor or bishop. It is often a hierarchical system with overseers at various levels above the local church. Although there may be local committees and councils that advise the pastor or bishop, decision-making and operation of ministry are, for the most part, at the discretion of a single individual. Many churches have variations of the episcopal system, but they all are distinguished by single-person preeminence at the local level and usually a variety of hierarchical structures above the local level.

When the term *congregational* is evoked in its broadest sense, it refers to the placing of authority of church government in the hands of members of the local assembly or congregation. Church boards usually run these churches. Although they have pastors, it is with a board gathered from among church members that the decision-making rests. The board not only gives direction but oversees the operation of the church. The pastor usually serves at the discretion of the board. These assemblies may be independent or have association with other church bodies, but they are autonomous in their local settings.

Whether we are talking about variations of the episcopal (one-man rule) or congregational (rule of the laity) governments, the church systems of man work against a multiplicity of ministry. Most Christian church government has been patterned after men's traditions made conspicuous by episcopal and congregational systems and not according to the Bible.

Not in any of the 48 mentioned churches of the New Testament was any church headed by a pastor or was anyone called "the pastor" of a church. Nor is there anywhere in the Bible that a board comprised of laity ruled a church. Yet in the modern Christian church, these are common manifestations of church government.

The New Testament does not say that a person with the pastor gifting should be the leader of a church. We name a leader who is in charge of a local church, "pastor," and expect him to meet every need of the "sheep," though he may be gifted in another facet of the fivefold ministry. The word *pastor* has been misused as a title. Both the ministry and the saints are lacking because of this improper use of church government.

This is not to say that using the title "pastor" is wrong. It is a term we all are familiar with. The error comes when a minister receives his position and authority from a title. The church fails to come into an order that would help it complete its purpose, if it ascribes titles in organizing the church that are not biblical. Titles provide great security for some, but their improper use also hinders proper understanding of church government.

After the reformation, the title "pastor" was first used for the local church leader. According to earlier religious traditions, ministry of the local church was vested in a single individual titled the pastor. A pastor in the fivefold ministry is one who personally cares for the people and tends to their needs; he is not necessarily the head of the local church. This single-faceted ministry of the church has become the best way for man to exert control, but it is not the biblical pattern. God's intent is to have the preeminence of the Holy Spirit rule the Church, and this can only come through a multiplicity of ministry.

*And the eye cannot say unto the hand, I have **no need** of thee: nor again the head to the feet, I have no need of you* (1 Corinthians 12:21, emphasis added).

*From whom the whole body fitly joined together and compacted by that which **every joint** supplieth, according to the effectual working in the measure of **every part**, maketh increase of the body unto the edifying of itself in love* (Ephesians 4:16, emphasis added).

The offices of apostle and prophet in many places are totally nonexistent; and where they may be recognized, as with the evangelist, they are often misapplications of their biblical purpose. Many churches feel they have no need of not only the total fivefold ministry but also the fullness of all biblical ministry. Unfortunately, the fullness of the ministry of the Body of Christ has not been manifested, in part, because only a small portion of the Body understands true ministry or is allowed to minister.

The ministry is often out of joint, which makes it difficult for the pastor to move the church in the ease and direction he sees the church should go. If every local church leader is literally a pastor in the fivefold ministry, where are the other ministry gifts? Well, God is shaking the Church out of its governmental complacency. He is showing all who will hear that there is a better way if only we are willing to lay aside our fears and preconceived ideas.

I am poured out like water, and all my bones are out of joint: my heart is like wax; it is melted in the midst of my bowels (Psalm 22:14).

The above verse is a messianic prophecy referring to the suffering of the Savior's body. It is also a foreshadowing of His Body to come—a Body that is in need of restoration. The Church today is out of joint and oppressed by those who should love it best. Only proper connection and order will allow the Body to minister in its purpose. The manifestation of the healthy Body of Christ will be in a multiplicity of ministry.

> *My praise shall be of Thee in the great congregation....All the ends of the world shall remember and turn unto the Lord: and all the kindreds of the nations shall worship before Thee. For the kingdom is the Lord's....A seed shall serve Him; it shall be accounted to the Lord for a generation* (Psalm 22:25,27-28,30).

The conclusion of Psalm chapter 22 states that a seed (remnant) will serve the Lord. The generation of the Lord is the manifested Body of Christ walking in the fullness of its ministry. Proper church government will order and direct the seed so that it can become the full manifestation of Jesus in the earth.

Ascension Gift Ministries

> *...He ascended up on high, He led captivity captive, and gave gifts unto men....And He gave some, apostles; and some, prophets; and some, evangelists; and some, pastors and teachers; for the perfecting of the saints, for the work of the ministry, for the edifying of the body of Christ: till we all come in the unity of the faith, and of the knowledge of the Son of God, unto a perfect man, unto the measure of the stature of the fullness of Christ* (Ephesians 4:8,11-13).

The ministry offices mentioned in the above Scriptures are often termed "ascension gift ministries." These ministries, as this Scripture indicates, are given to the Church for three primary purposes: 1) the perfecting of the saints; 2) the work of the ministry (literally the saints ministry); and 3) the edification of the Body. This entire responsibility has often been vested in one man, but it is impossible for any single person to properly complete the ministry belonging to all the offices.

To receive extra help, the pastor often assigns tasks to certain committees, or churches may establish boards, but they are no substitute for the "ascension gift ministries." In fact, these committees and boards can and sometimes do work against the establishment of proper ministry government. The pastor in a modern church organization is often expected and required to be all things to the church.

Even though his God-given gift may not function in every area, he is often expected to be preacher, counselor, teacher, administrator, prophet, financial officer, theologian, chief executive officer, and much more to the local church. Obviously, it is totally unrealistic to place this variety of responsibilities into the hands of a single individual. God gives grace to whatever gift ministry He establishes.

If we limit ministry in the local church to the pastor or bishop calling, we miss the fullness of the ministry gifts to the church. We may recognize certain individuals as being evangelists or prophets, but that is not the same as having their governmental office in operation in the church. All five ascension gift ministries were given to the church. All five are needed in the church to receive the fullness of the ministry of the Holy Spirit. Unfortunately, a single ministry office has usurped the authority of the apostle, prophet, true evangelist, pastor, and teacher; and this inappropriate rule has caused a tremendous lack within the Body.

If a pastor tries to function in areas beyond his gifting, he will labor without the grace of God. Grace always fits the gift. We should not expect God's grace in an area that He has not chosen to gift us. We may acknowledge the presence of the five-fold ministry, but that is not the same as establishing these offices within the local church. The hesitancy of establishing these offices often lays in a fear of the pastor or bishop losing control, influence, and rule.

There will be, and frankly needs to be, a loss of control; this control will not be given over to men, but to the Spirit. A ministry that needs to control everyone and everything operates in fear and is actually out of control. We gain true control when the Spirit is in control; only proper government allows for this possibility. Influence and rule will then increase. Multiplicity does not decrease, but vastly increases not only the power and strength of the church but also of every ministry within that church.

But unto every one of us is given grace according to the measure of the gift of Christ (Ephesians 4:7).

If all callings are allowed to operate in the local church, then there will be grace for every gift to function in its fullness. If it is understood that the other areas of ministry are also needed to complete God's order, we will avoid the problem of restricted and ingrown ministry. Ministry is burning out, not because it has too much opposition or is confronted with too many problems, but because it lacks the proper governmental order. If we are in order, then His yoke is easy and His burden light.

Most churches operate via single-man rule. Some have established boards, which are found nowhere in Scripture. Others are controlled from a headquarters that places and removes pastors at will. In some systems, the reward for years of church planting and nurturing becomes a personal kingdom of sorts ruled by the pastor. Because he has put in the effort to build the work, he receives the reward independent from any other influence. Again, these situations lack proper biblical government.

Some pastors greatly fear the establishment of a multiplicity of ministry, for they perceive it to be a potential threat to their control and their right to rule as well as a potential loss of their finances. Although proper biblical ministry will challenge the control of a single individual, the actual authority and power of not only the church but also the pastor will be greatly increased by a multiplicity of ministry.

Ministries desiring the progressive move of God have increasingly realized existing structures will never bring this to pass. Instead, what is needed is an understanding of God's church government. It is possible to list many requirements and responsibilities in a job description, but there is an ascension gift calling that the leader's spirit majors in, for which he has grace, and outside of which he is clumsy and does not function well. Working outside the grace of God can even lead to moral and physical breakdown. It is very important that every church leader recognize which of the ascension gifts he operates in, so he can allow himself to be surrounded with others who have giftings and offices that he lacks. When this occurs, that church will receive the entire ministry God has for them.

The operation of the five-faceted ascension gift ministries are not only vital for the church, but provide liberty and support for the individual operating in the traditional pastor's role. The present organization of the Church will never bring Kingdom rule. A multiplicity, however, will not only bring the rule of the Spirit in greater measures, but a freedom and peace to those presently struggling under a system of man's government.

Describing the Fivefold Ministry

The apostle governs. The prophet guides—points the way. The evangelist gathers. The pastor/shepherd guards or cares for the sheep. The teacher grounds or establishes. But under traditional religious organization, the pastor or bishop acts as the apostle, prophet, evangelist, pastor, and teacher. He ascribes all aspects of the fivefold ministry to himself and thus dwells among his people as the earthly representative of God. Although it would not likely be admitted, he often becomes the mediator between God and the local church.

Wherefore He saith, When He ascended up on high, He led captivity captive, and gave gifts unto men. (Now that He ascended, what is it but that He also descended first into the lower parts of the earth? He that descended is the same also that ascended up far above all heavens, that He might fill all things) (Ephesians 4:8-10).

Jesus transposed His person into the Body of Christ in the form of gifts to men. He gifted men with facets of Himself. He had the Spirit without measure, but He gives the Spirit by measure, thus we have a portion of Him in His gifting to us. The only way that Jesus can be completely manifest is in the fullness of His Body. For this to happen requires the coming together of the various gifts given to individual members within the church. If they do not come together, and if all those with rule do not govern in the office given them, then we will witness only a portion of Christ.

The chariots of God are twenty thousand, even thousands of angels: the Lord is among them, as in Sinai, in the holy place (Psalm 68:17).

In God's system, there is a many-faceted ministry universally made up of a multiple of ministers. Whereas in the episcopal system, it is often assumed that whoever is the leader, in other words the pastor of the church, represents the totality of deity as to government for the entire congregation. This caste system of pastor (whether a saint or appointed by a church board) divides the Body of Christ.

When meeting other Christians, where they attend church is a question that often takes precedence over who they are in God. We classify people according to titles or the name of their church and, thus, rarely relate to them according to what their purpose is or the vision that God has given them. People feel comfortable when they feel they have things figured out. The natural mind desires the security of titles. It is normal for us to categorize and pigeonhole others. On the other hand, the spiritual mind is not impressed by titles but is moved by the witness and power of the Holy Spirit.

Many may be confused in establishing a multiplicity of ministry, for it is not the way they have been accustomed to seeing the Church operate. This is why it is wise not to get ahead of the Holy Spirit in trying to establish a multiplicity. People need time, preparation, and teaching. A pastor should never try to bring forth a multiplicity out of frustration because of present situations, but only by the witness of the Holy Spirit with a clear understanding and patience to allow God to prepare both him and the people.

Churches have sometimes become gnarled and ingrown because they have been exposed to only one facet of the ministry. Instead of having the fullness of God dwelling among them, they have a mere one-fifth of Him or less, or have an improper mixture of ministry. They have not seen the other characteristics of God, which come through gifted men and women, manifesting the many facets of Himself, where His character, power, vision, love, will, and purpose are thus understood.

The set ministry is obligated from time to time to bring in those gifted to minister in the areas that are lacking. Just as no saint is an island in Christianity, so no local church is an island that has no need of any other part of the greater Body of Christ. We need relationship among saints, and we also need relationship among churches.

This helps keep a church from becoming ingrown and self-focused, and equally important allows the unique position and vision of each individual church to be benefited by the others. Each local church has a unique purpose and position in the overall plan of God. The Church for the most part has not recognized this, because it is uninformed about its true purpose and power. For the most part, all local churches are thought of as playing the same part in God's plan and only seldom are thought of as having their own uniqueness and special purpose.

> *And God hath set some in the church, first apostles, secondarily prophets, thirdly teachers, after that miracles* (1 Corinthians 12:28a).

God sets an order in each local church, and there is a purpose for each church. If the pastor and church ministry do not properly understand who they are to the local church, the saints within the church will not properly understand or manifest who they are to the community. A multiplicity will bring this clarity.

New and Old Testament Ministry Order

Let all things be done decently and in order (1 Corinthians 14:40).

We often try to fit a revived, renewed church into an old "wineskin," but attempting to put a new move or revelation of God into an old church government will not work. We need to return to the New Testament and understand the order of church government ministered through the apostles and elders.

God ordained the high priests, priests, and Levites in the Old Testament. In the New Testament, He gave apostles, elders, and deacons to the Church—the New Testament counterparts to the Old Testament offices mentioned above. The Levites, equivalent to our deacons, waited on the house of the Lord, serving by doing the physical work. The priests offered sacrifices for themselves and the people, which is a pattern of our eldership.

The high priest had the responsibility of oversight in a chosen area so that God's requirements were met in that place for His purpose. Thus, the apostle governs. This apostolic ministry is the ministry of the set man. If we plan to see a great harvesting and networking, we need to come into the New Testament order of church government by leaving the old system that was borrowed from men who did not know true revival or restoration.

God's ministry in the Bible is often revealed in the number five. Five is the number of grace through ministry. There is the fivefold ministry of apostle, prophet, evangelist, pastor, and teacher. Aaron and his four sons made up the original ministry under Moses. In Isaiah 9:6, the fullness of Christ's ministry is found in five attributes: the government on the shoulder, wonderful, counselor, mighty God, and prince of peace. Abraham's vision also gives this pattern of fivefold ministry.

> *And He said unto him, Take me an heifer of three years old, and a she goat of three years old, and a ram of three years old, and a turtledove, and a young pigeon. And he took unto Him all these, and divided them in the midst, and laid each piece one against another: but the birds divided he not* (Genesis 15:9-10).

Abraham wanted to know with certainty that he would inherit the land. God told him to make a particular sacrifice that would confirm this to him. The sacrifice typified the fivefold ministry. The answer to Abraham's dream about bondage of his people would come as a result of this type of ministry that Abraham was to protect and watch over until its completion. The five animals of the sacrifice can be considered as follows:

1. *Heifer*: One untried that is sent looking for mating. It is the apostle spirit that goes out and searches—one sent.

2. *She-goat*: Type of pastor, giving milk to the kids even in mountainous and rough places.

3. *Ram*: Leading the flock and giving direction to the flock—prophet.

4. *Turtle Dove: "When He, the Spirit of truth, is come, He will guide you into all truth"* (Jn. 16:13a). The Spirit descended on Jesus as a dove—the Spirit to teach—the dove is the Teacher.

5. *Pigeon:* The carrier that takes news—the evangelist.

God walked among these sacrifices and made covenant with Abraham by blood. Each sacrifice was put against the other—not separated, but in order. The ministry must not be separated. The sacrifices were cut open—made transparent. Ministry must be transparent, as well, with no hidden agendas, not seeking its own. They were cut open and laid against one another—ministry needs connection and has to work together.

In the evening, the vultures came—a type of the end of an era. The prey must be beaten off the sacrifice until the going down of the sun. A church in proper multiplicity order will have the vultures beaten off of leadership by those near who want to see the establishment of the land. The people and the ministry work together and function together for the fulfillment of the plan of God.

Changes in church government can be very traumatic; therefore, the plan and purpose of God should be sought and implemented with patience. The leader should surround himself with wise, godly counselors (a presbytery) who share his vision and burden. The Bible says, *"In the multitude of counselors there is safety"* (Prov. 11:14)—not in the multitude of advisors, but in individuals with peer standing who bring gifting and insight, not necessarily possessed by the set ministry.

What God wants to do should be birthed in the set ministry. There must be courage to remove or change what hinders God's work from progressing, but it needs to be done in God's timing and according to His instruction with His grace upon it.

Chapter Seven

THE OPERATION
OF THE
FIVE-FACETED MINISTRY

God wishes to be Lord over His Church, and He wants to dwell among His people. He has given the five-faceted gift to the Church through chosen individuals; and when we receive these in their gift and office, we receive Him. It takes all facets of the God-given ministry to bring the Church into perfection. Otherwise, the congregation will be self-willed without an apostle, blind without a prophet, ingrown without an evangelist, numb without a teacher, and a spoiled congregation if they have only the pastor gifting. When any one of these is lacking, a part of Christ is lacking.

The Set Ministry

The set man surrounds himself with the fivefold ministry so the Church can be perfected. Each ministry represents only one small facet of what God really is. Many times problems develop in the lives of leaders because they are overworked and are asked to give more than they possess. They should not be criticized, because it is the system that needs to be changed. When their time is filled with a multitude of duties outside their calling, they cannot possibly fulfill the ministry God has called them to do.

And God hath set some in the church, first apostles, secondarily prophets, thirdly teachers, after that miracles, then gifts of healings, helps, governments, diversities of tongues (1 Corinthians 12:28).

The Interaction of the Five-Faceted Ministry

The apostle establishes government, which provides a foundation to build on. Then a prophet brings vision of what God wants to build on that foundation. Next, the teacher establishes the people in the Word, raising up godly ministers from among them who can help lead the church. After that, evangelism and pastoring provides care, nurturing, and outreach. All these aspects of the ministry are needed.

The set minister's gifting may be any of the five-faceted ministry gifts, but in his position of rule, he will be an apostle to the local church. The set ministry is a ministry of foundation and establishment. By providing godly vision and foundation, he establishes a base upon which a multiplicity can be built. Paul was called an apostle after he was sent forth from the Antioch church to establish foundations for new churches. Although he operated at times in one or more of the five-faceted ministry giftings, he had the measure or rule of an apostle. The person whom God calls over the work is set by God and functions as an apostle whether he is an apostle by calling or has another ministry gift.

There are *doma* gifts and *charismatic* gifts in the Bible. A set minister could be a teacher and yet operate under his doma gift as an apostle. Doma gifting is the gifting of our measure of rule. If the church is not in order, people may be drawn by the preaching or the miraculous, but they will have a difficult time being established in their ministry or purpose. The Old Testament is a schoolmaster to bring us to Christ. It contains a pattern of how ministry should function.

And Moses spake unto the Lord, saying, Let the Lord, the God of the spirits of all flesh, set a man over the congregation, which may go out before them, and which may go in before them, and which may lead them out, and which may bring them in; that the congregation of the Lord be not as sheep which have no shepherd (Numbers 27:15-17).

God desires to sovereignly set headship in the Church; but existing church structures, our fears, and traditions impede His will. The process of many churches is to democratically vote for whom they want or to have leaders appointed by a denominational hierarchy. *"Having itching ears,"* they decide who is to be their leader so what is preached will please the people or satisfy the needs of the organization but not necessarily complete God's purpose. Leaders chosen for their personality, preaching ability, or personal acquaintances, and not according to biblical pattern, may lack the grace, understanding, or rule to implement God's vision for that locale.

Local church boards are a man-designated substitute for the proper authority of God in running the church and choosing ministry. Under a multiplicity, all in church who qualify through training and maturity have opportunity to minister. The question is whether ministry will follow a biblical pattern or a man-made order. Rule by the people instead of rule by God's ordained authority will not bring forth a Kingdom order.

God hates rule by laity in the Church because it places people in the position of God—deciding for themselves who will be their teacher, what they will be taught, and how the church will operate. This rule was never sanctioned by God in His Word. This type of church government seldom allows for proper correction, edification, or strength, because it is outside the order of God.

Without proper order, it is difficult to go from glory to glory or from faith to faith. Since proper correction is limited by the laity's control, many times the rebellious and gossips control the church. Instead of being led by a pastor set by God, they are led by their understanding of what God would want. Some even go so far as to dictate to the pastor what should be taught or spoken. The Church should not be a democracy that is governed by the people, but a theocracy that is governed by God.

Only a church established upon a multiplicity will allow for the proper ministry of all the people and the rule of the Spirit. God wants to speak in edification and correction, revealing Himself and His will to man. He wants to look at us in all our need and raise us up in all His glory. He wants to be the head of the Church.

But now hath God set the members every one of them in the body, as it hath pleased Him (1 Corinthians 12:18).

God alone knows what we need because He is the God of the spirits of all flesh. God calls and sets the apostle and elders in the church and gives them authority to rule. The set leader does not have to be a pastor in the fivefold ministry; and if he is not, he needs to surround himself with a pastor as well as the other fivefold ministry gifts.

Elders and Evangelists

Elders are overseers of the church and are ordained in the local church by set ministry. They are given responsibility to watch over the work in a particular area. Working together, they provide the multifaceted ministry needed to complete the plan of God.

The multiple ministries of the set man and elders will pastor the church—each providing ministerial care for the people according to their position with the set minister as the head. The apostle Peter said he was an elder, which means pastor or shepherd. The growth of eldership in a church depends on the growth and need of the church, as well as the set man's ability to teach and raise up people into the ministry. Once a local church had reached a certain maturity and level of governance, it was the apostle Paul's decree that elders be ordained in every city.

The spirit of an evangelist should also be resident in the church so there is a continual adding to the church and through the church. The evangelist is not just an itinerate preacher who visits the local church to stir up the lost in the community, thereby adding new members to the church. The ministry of the evangelist should be a continuing, integral part of every local church.

Presbytery and Passing on Authority

Churches need a presbytery of God-gifted and established ministries outside the local church, who can be called upon when the set minister senses that something is lacking. They are not a board of people but rather carefully chosen ministers whose hearts and visions are joined with the church in a unity of purpose and understanding. A presbytery or set ministry council composed of true elders of the Church of God are not only a protection, strength, and council for the Church, but also for the set ministry.

Godly young ministers need to be taught and raised up in the atmosphere of the local church—receiving the attitude, spirit and heart of the set man. Every church should be a Bible school. Instead of being trained in someone else's vision, young ministers and saints need the vision of their own local church. They need to be raised in the vision of the set minister and take on part of his ministry. Ministry is not singular, but plural. Joshua is an example of this pattern. He was a servant and a close follower of Moses. His right to lead came from his position in God and his relationship to the ministry of Moses.

*And the Lord said unto Moses, Take thee Joshua the son of Nun, a man **in whom is the spirit,** and lay thine hand upon him; and set him before Eleazar the priest, and before all the congregation; and give him a charge in their sight. And thou shalt put some of thine honour upon him, that all the congregation of the children of Israel may be obedient. And he shall stand before Eleazar the priest, who shall ask counsel for him after the judgment of Urim before the Lord: at his word shall they go out, and at his word they shall come in, both he, and all the children of Israel with him, even all the congregation* (Numbers 27:18-21, emphasis added).

"In whom is the spirit" in the original text has a possessive tense—*"in whom is thy spirit."* God told Moses to find a man with the same spirit as he had to be set over the congregation. In the same manner, Elijah said to Elisha, *"If you see eye to eye with me when I go away, then a double portion of my spirit will be upon you."* The set man finds a God-gifted person who is in agreement with his spirit to whom he can give honor and authority. A presbytery of ministry and the congregation are gathered to confirm him.

Those who would minister together should all be thoroughly taught the same thing and made Kingdom-conscious, so they will serve one another and not themselves. They must realize they are saved by grace for God's purpose.

A minister needs to understand the principle of spiritual authority, or he will tear down the work of the Kingdom not understanding his relationship to God's authority and to the authority of the set man.

People need to be taught to care for others, for leadership, and for God's truth. When they gain this consciousness of the Kingdom of God and seek the Kingdom first, they can be trusted in positions of authority. The vision that God gives for a particular church begins with the set man. This vision is then taught to the people, which brings unity to the Body.

Ministries Surrounding the Set Man

Now there were in the church that was at Antioch certain prophets and teachers (Acts 13:1a).

The ministries surrounding the set man should guard him and his vision. He touches every ministry and every ministry touches him. An elder should look for faithful people with ability who can expand the work of the ministry and further the vision so the work of God will grow. The administration of a church should not be seen as just business but should be directed by God-gifted ministry. Many decisions concerning the church should be made through Elders who are ordained from various ministry giftings to minister in that gift to the church.

People of ministry should do the work of the church. Even secretaries should be spiritual, trained in the work of God. People who are placed in positions need to have the same vision as the set man and be dedicated to God's Kingdom and not their own. Unless people understand they were saved for purpose, they will never be brought to maturity but be perpetual spiritual babies. The Apostle Paul was chosen for the purpose of writing a major part of the New Testament as well as leading many to Christ. An individual is saved for the purpose of bringing his whole family to God. People are saved to serve God by serving others.

The Establishing of Elders

Eldership is like the fingers on a hand—it is generally made up of the five-faceted ministry gifts spoken of in previous chapters. Eldership is God's vehicle for implementation of His plan and purpose in the Church.

Humble yourselves therefore under the mighty hand of God, that He may exalt you in due time (1 Peter 5:6).

God's plan is to extend His mighty hand in the earth through His gifted ministry. Their purpose is to reflect the glory of God in the earth. This is done through their diversity, not through sameness. As a cut prism catches different points of light and reflects each in distinct colors, diversity in ministry shows us different aspects of God.

Types of Eldership and Set Ministry in the Old Testament

As mentioned previously, the apostle locates the place and purpose of God's work. The prophet speaks forth direction from God for that place. Then on that foundation, the Teacher can teach the promise of God. The ministry of Moses and the elders can be compared to the apostle and elders. The high priest, priests, and Levites are patterns of the apostle, elders, and deacons.

Hearken now unto my voice, I will give thee counsel, and God shall be with thee: be thou for the people to God-ward, that thou mayest bring the causes unto God: and thou shalt teach them ordinances and laws, and shalt show them the way wherein they must walk, and the work that they must do. Moreover thou shalt provide out of all the people able men, such as fear God, men of truth, hating covetousness; and place such over them, to be rulers of thousands, and rulers of hundreds, rulers of fifties, and rulers of tens: and let them judge the people at all seasons: and it shall be, that every great matter they shall bring unto thee, but every small matter they shall judge: so shall it be easier for thyself, and they shall bear the burden with thee. If thou shalt do this thing, and God command thee so, then thou shalt be able to endure, and all this people shall also go to their place in peace. So Moses hearkened to the voice of his father-in-law, and did all that he had said. And Moses chose able men out of all Israel, and made them heads over the people, rulers of thousands, rulers of hundreds, rulers of fifties, and rulers of tens. And they judged the people at all seasons: the hard causes they brought unto Moses, but every small matter they judged themselves (Exodus 18:19-26).

Jethro was a priest of God in Midian and father-in-law to Moses, who gave godly counsel to Moses concerning eldership (see Ex. 18:13-26). Jethro said that it was not good for Moses to govern alone, for his own sake and for the sake of the people. He advised Moses to be toward God (receive the vision from God) and to choose men to minister to the people. A leader must have time alone with God. He cannot be God-ward if he is constantly toward the people. Elders help the set ministry by overseeing the flock so the set minister can be God-ward for the people.

Exodus 18:21 lists necessary characteristics of elders. There are four essentials for qualification of eldership, and all four must be present in anyone chosen: 1) Elders in Israel were to be able men—God-gifted men with ability; 2) They were to be men who feared God and understood spiritual authority, meaning they obeyed God and whoever He had placed in authority; 3) They were to be men of truth. They were to have no personal motives or agenda but were to be transparent, having pure honesty. 4) Finally, they were to hate covetousness, having no jealousy, not wanting someone else's job or desiring to take over something not appointed for them.

The Jews knew very well the function of eldership from the study of the Old Testament and the practice of it in their time. There must be headship established, but the ministry must be one of multiplicity. Eldership must be vested in more than just the pastor. Elders are not just helpers for the pastor's ministry, but overseers who lend their specific gifting and unique ministries to the greater ministry of the

Body. Our understanding, and not necessarily the titles, needs to change. Regardless of whether or not we use the titles of pastor or bishop or prophet, the offices and ministry of the local church need to reflect God's biblical order of a multiplicity of ministry.

Distinctions in Ministry Gifts

The Bible says that all can prophesy, but this does not mean that everyone holds the office of a prophet. All the leadership can pastor and care for "sheep," but that does not mean they all have the God-given office of a pastor in the fivefold ministry. Many can teach, but each one does not operate in the office of teacher.

God gives spiritual gifts to all, but He appoints only some to particular offices of authority. This is the distinction between charisma and doma gifting. The fivefold ministry gifts of Ephesians chapter 4 are doma gifts, meaning they are offices of rule. Whereas, the gifts of Romans chapter 12 are charisma gifts that are given to each Christian by the Spirit according to His purpose for their life. Charisma gifts are part of who we are, and they are in us even prior to salvation, even though their full exercise may only manifest in service to God.

Everyone has been given charisma gifts, but not everyone has doma gifting which manifests itself in offices of authority. Due to the immaturity of the Church most recognize and seek charisma gifts, but few are able to appreciate or recognize ministries of rule. This is one reason the Church is so lacking in foundation and godly direction.

Those in ministry may flow in a variety of gifting from time to time. Even though Timothy was called an apostle and an elder, Paul told him to do the work of an evangelist in a certain place because of the need. However, just because he did the work of an evangelist at that time, does not mean that he held the office of an evangelist. In the same manner, if someone prophesies, that does not necessarily make them a prophet; they are simply operating a gift of the spirit called prophecy, for that particular time.

The man God sets in a place operates under an apostolic doma gift. He should then train others to minister and should provide people to care for the congregation. He should help define their gifting, ministry, and call. The ones who should fill positions in the Church are those whom God has gifted and called for particular areas of service. But because this order is lacking, saints are confused about who they are and what their purpose is. The set man should seek for the confirmation of the Holy Spirit concerning the appointment of eldership, and then bring them before the apostles and elders for confirmation—a presbytery of ministry who are set in order

According to the Book of Acts, deacons need to be full of the Holy Spirit and wisdom. They are placed in the position of deacon because of their gifting and readiness to serve. There should be one vision—the vision of the set ministry that he has personally received from God for that particular church. All people in that local church must come under that vision. Therefore, if anyone has an opposing vision, that vision is either not from God, or they should be set elsewhere. Contrary visions will always bring division in a church. If anyone is in disagreement with the vision of the house and cannot submit to that vision and those entrusted with its care, he should leave and find a place that shares his same vision.

It is worth repeating that when it comes to choosing a church, most people look for good preaching, church programs that minister to their needs, a convenient location, a church that a friend may attend, or one that is of a particular denomination. However, none of the above criteria are good reasons to join a local church. "The people seem so loving"; "The pastor seems so nice"; "They really believe in the Word" are not necessarily reasons to connect to a local church.

Since many Christians have never been taught to hear the voice of God, they instead seek peripheral signs and reasons in their choice of a church. But the only right reason to become connected to a people is because God has spoken it to you. If God has truly spoken it to you, then it will be easy for you to be in agreement with and supportive of the vision in that place—assuming they have a clear godly vision. If you cannot be submitted to the vision of the house, then God did not call you there.

It is from the vision that your purpose, unity, and ministry will come. If after proper prayer and instruction you still are not in agreement with the vision, you do not belong in that house. Find a house of your vision in which you can submit to the authority and not bring division into that place.

Being Under Authority—the Key to Acquiring Authority

People in the Armed Forces are under authority and guard our entire nation by precisely following their given orders. The centurion in Jesus' time said that he was a man under authority. He understood its function and recognized that Jesus was also under authority. Jesus had authority to speak the Word and that Word would be obeyed—and the centurion's servant would be healed.

> *For I also am a man set under authority, having under me soldiers, and I say unto one, Go, and he goeth; and to another, Come, and he cometh; and to my servant, Do this, and he doeth it. When Jesus heard these things, he marvelled at him, and turned him about, and said unto the people that followed Him, I say unto you, I have not found so great faith, no, not in Israel* (Luke 7:8-9).

Jesus called this centurion an example of "great faith." He had great faith because he understood authority, and that at its root all authority is based on submission. Only those under authority have the right or ability to exercise proper authority.

124

Those who do not understand spiritual authority will destroy the church by following their own will instead of the God-given vision. The headship is anointed when each person honors the authority directly above him until it reaches the highest level. In turn, the blessings can then flow all the way down. A person honors God by honoring his immediate authority. However, God cannot be honored if the authorities He has put in place are ignored.

Even though able men and women are needed in church, people coming from other churches should not be taken in quickly without the eldership knowing their background and who their father is so that it can be determined if they have a right to minister. If someone has caused division in another church, he or she will probably cause division again, unless they learn to submit properly to authority.

After Elijah was taken up and a prophet was needed, Elisha his servant, who had poured water on the hands of Elijah, became that prophet. The king said, *"The word of the Lord is with him"* (2 Kings 3:12a; see also 3:11). The leader to replace Moses was found in his servant Joshua, who had the spirit of Moses in him. A person who has faithfully followed, served, and received the spirit of the set man, may be the one who God ordains to succeed him. This is exemplified in Jesus and His followers as well.

An outside presbytery of three to five, proven, loving, Kingdom-conscious ministries needs to surround the local eldership. They should have a similar vision and be united by God with the spirit of the local church. This presbytery is especially helpful for the smaller church that does not yet contain the fivefold ministry, because they help fill the void until these ministries come forth in the church.

Chapter Eight

---·••·•---

THE REQUIREMENT
OF SPIRITUAL
IMPLEMENTATION

It is difficult for many people in ministry to accurately appraise the true spiritual success of their ministry. Our gauge seldom equates to His. Some would use a worldly standard measuring their accomplishment according to how the ministry is accepted by the world or its impact upon the world. Others would use a business formula that would cite as evidence of successful ministry such things as building programs, size of the congregation, income, or ministry outreaches. Still others would use a personal standard of judging the effectiveness of ministry by the numbers "reached for Christ" or by some other measure of personal achievement.

Now all these can be viewed in some degree as "spiritual" measurements, yet those who strive for the excellency of father/son order have learned that success of ministry can only be measured as Jesus measured His own ministry.

It is finished... (Jn. 19:30b).

Of them which thou gavest Me have I lost none (Jn. 18:9b).

True ministry fathers know the only measurement in assessing the success of ministry is: Have I done the will of God by completing the vision, and have I ordered those sons that He gave me? Jesus taught more revelation, walked in more power, saved more souls, healed more sick people, and performed more miracles than any man of God in all history. At times, He used these as confirmation of His ministry, but never as a measurement of success.

What constitutes spiritual success can be argued. What standard do we use to gauge such success, and is it even important to do so? Paul, in Second Corinthians, gives the measure of those who lack wisdom: *"For we dare not make ourselves of the number, or compare ourselves with some that commend themselves: but they measuring themselves by themselves, and comparing themselves among themselves, are not wise"* (2 Cor. 10:12). Unfortunately, this is a standard all too often used by ministry in evaluating and assessing its success. The unwise always use a mark other than Christ to gauge their successes and failures.

The apostle Paul was continually gauging the success of His ministry as marked against the vision and work of God and the measure of Christ: *"I count all things but loss for the excellency of the knowledge of Christ Jesus my Lord: for whom I have suffered the loss of all things, and do count them but dung, that I may win Christ....I have fought a good fight, I have finished my course* [the vision], *I have kept the faith"* (Phil. 3:8; 2 Tim. 4:7). And finally, before King Agrippa the summation of His ministry was: *"I was not disobedient unto the heavenly vision"* (Acts 26:19b).

We need to do likewise so that we can make adjustments in our ministries to bring them into perfected order. Ours is not a measurement gauged against others' achievements or opinions, but against the vision God gave us and the care for the people He entrusted to us.

Successful ministry can seldom be measured by material acquisition, nor can the Kingdom be measured in dollars and cents. In the natural world, fortunes have been amassed by individuals under a variety of circumstances. Some have inherited great wealth while others have acquired it through dishonest and corrupt means, and even others have had the fortune to discover an oil well in their backyard. The majority of people who possess wealth, though, have obtained it through a process of hard work, skill, and dedication.

In any case, no matter how wealth has been acquired, the mere possession of wealth is no measurement as to the character or genius of the one who possesses it. "Prosperity" is not necessarily a mark of successful ministry. On the other hand, Christian ministry is not wise if it does not assess its effectiveness, or if it does so by comparisons with other ministries and not by its unique vision given from God.

There Is a Wide Gulf Between
Spiritual Understanding and Spiritual Implementation

Spiritual understanding requires knowledge, submission, and right questioning; while spiritual implementation requires wisdom, preparation, dedication, and order. There have been many powerful ministries who understood what God wanted of them but were never quite able to implement what they understood.

> *Through wisdom is an house builded; and by understanding it is established: and by knowledge shall the chambers be filled with all precious and pleasant riches* (Proverbs 24:3-4).

God desires to build us a spiritual house and to build us into a spiritual house. We are the spiritual habitation of the Lord. We are His dwelling place.

> *The Lord telleth thee that He will make thee an house* (2 Samuel 7:11b).

> *Ye also, as lively stones, are built up a spiritual house* (1 Peter 2:5a).

Spiritual *under*standing or that which forms the foundation under which we stand, always requires the knowledge of God. This knowledge is not just about what God knows, but also concerns what we need to know about God. In addition to knowledge, understanding requires submission and asking the right questions. Submission, properly understood, is the fear of the Lord. Some of the most studied ministries walk with little understanding because they have never disciplined themselves to manifest proper submission.

Without valid father/son relationship, how will a ministry ever exemplify proper submission or honor? Desire, right motives, and a pure heart are the wellspring from which come right questions. Often, people with great knowledge lack understanding because they don't know how to ask the right questions that will bring forth understanding from the knowledge they possess.

Spiritual implementation is the ability to take a vision from God and bring it to pass in the earth. Spiritual implementation or putting into operation the things we understand in the Spirit requires a different set of criteria than that of spiritual understanding. It is out of wisdom, dedication, preparation, and order that spiritual implementation comes.

If a ministry has problems implementing what they clearly understand the Lord has given them, then the problem is likely to be found in one of the previously mentioned four areas: Wisdom—the Holy Spirit-directed application of knowledge and understanding; dedication—consecrated to a godly course regardless of fleshly distractions and desires; preparation—what is done beforehand to make what comes after it prosper; order—being in the placement, timing, and plan of God so that His Spirit has free course to operate.

Prepare ye the way of the Lord... (Isaiah 40:3b)

...prepare ye the way of the people (Isaiah 62:10a).

God calls us to prepare because our ability to be used by Him is largely dependent upon preparation. Order is conforming to the plan of God. Father/son order is one such plan of God. How can we fully implement vision without coming into order?

The Ministry of Jesus

Jesus' ministry displayed both great understanding and great spiritual implementation. Jesus had a plan for everything He did. It was not a haphazard ministry deciding at the dawn of each day what should come next.

And Jesus increased in wisdom and stature, and in favour with God and man (Luke 2:52).

Jesus used wisdom and prepared Himself. At 12 years of age, He knew His identity and purpose because He was submitted to His Father. The fact that these characteristics increased in Jesus speaks of preparation. There was a time when Jesus had more wisdom than He had previously. Yes, even Jesus was prepared and grew in maturity.

"As his custom was, He went into the synagogue on the sabbath day, and stood up for to read" (Lk. 4:16, emphasis added). Jesus had a custom, a routine or plan He followed in how He ministered.

"He humbled Himself, and became obedient unto death, even the death of the cross" (Phil. 2:8b). Jesus was totally submitted to the Father, and this helped bring forth His great understanding.

"And saith unto them, Go your way into the village over against you: and as soon as ye be entered into it, ye shall find a colt tied, whereon never man sat; loose him, and bring him" (Mk. 11:2). Jesus had prepared even the seemingly insignificant details so that His ministry might be made complete.

"And He must needs go through Samaria" (Jn. 4:4).
Nothing was left to chance in His ministry. He
understood what He needed to do and how to do it.

*"And it came to pass, when the time was come that He
should be received up, He stedfastly set His face to go to
Jerusalem"* (Lk. 9:51). He entertained no distractions.
He was totally dedicated and ordered His ministry to
complete the vision given from His Father.

One of the chief ways Jesus ordered His ministry was in
the call and appointment of His apostles. Jesus ordered His
ministry according to the pattern given by God through
Moses. He didn't look for a new plan or a more effective plan;
but because He had understanding, He followed a plan given
by the Father, for it was a perfect plan and a type of that which
His Father would do through Him in the Spirit.

*And had a wall great and high, and had twelve gates, and
at the gates twelve angels, and names written thereon,
which are the names of the twelve tribes of the children of
Israel* (Revelation 21:12).

*And the wall of the city had twelve foundations, and in
them the names of the twelve apostles of the Lamb*
(Revelation 21:14).

*And the Lord said unto Moses, Gather unto Me seventy
men of the elders of Israel, whom thou knowest to be the
elders of the people, and officers over them; and bring
them unto the tabernacle of the congregation, that they
may stand there with thee* (Numbers 11:16).

*After these things the Lord appointed other seventy also,
and sent them two and two before His face into every city
and place, whither He Himself would come* (Luke 10:1).

Jesus chose 12 (signifying foundation and government)
apostles. He also chose 70 (7 x 10, perfection times order) and

sent them out two by two. These 70 are like the eldership of the Church (see Num. 11:25). He also had many other disciples (servants—by implication, the deacons). Likewise, the Jewish religion in Jesus' day was organized after Old Testament patterns. He followed the pattern of the high priest office, the Sanhedrin—or the council of elders, and the temple ministry.

Jesus didn't say (as many religious people of our day), "I have all these people, and I want to give them each a job so they feel part of My ministry." Instead, He had a preestablished plan from the Father and the understanding to implement it. The patriarchs of Israel became a pattern for the number of His apostles. The 70 elders called by Moses became the model for the 70 called and sent out by Jesus.

The apostles were ministry sons of Jesus. They gave Him relationship and provided service, and He entrusted the care of His ministry into their hands. In fact, were it not for the training and relationship they received from Jesus, Jesus' ministry would not have survived beyond His death. Jesus was totally dependent on these ministry sons to carry the message and order of His ministry to the world.

Yet today, what appear to be great ministries of God will end at the gravesite or be perverted by those who come after because ministry fails to bring forth *genuine* ministry sons in *proper* order. Many people in ministry today seek to emulate Jesus' power, fame, and miracles, but few want to imitate His selfless service to His Father and His servanthood toward mankind. They desire to eat His flesh, but they are unwilling to drink His blood. If we are willing to eat and live off the revelation and Word given by the Spirit, we also need to be willing to become partakers of His suffering and sacrifice.

And when it was day, he called unto Him His disciples: and of them He chose twelve, whom also He named apostles (Luke 6:13).

The apostles were first disciples. There was some qualification and preparation necessary for this calling. They were disciples first. There is also a plan for those the Father would bring into our ministries. He certainly chooses some we would discard. He also chooses some who may not be genuine but fulfill His greater purpose. Paul had Demas and of course Jesus had Judas. God knows what we do not and brings His will to pass.

In ordering His ministry with the 12, Jesus chose at least four sets of brothers. He chose fishermen, married and single men, tax collectors, a political insurrectionist, and even a thief. He did not seek the prominent or prosperous or even the socially acceptable, but for those given Him by the Father. It was not His will but the Father's that He sought.

Because the Lord looks at the heart, He sees value in people that our prejudices and fears often overlook. He sees in His sons not only what they are, but more importantly, what they can become. He's not afraid to bring into His ministry those who are less than perfect, knowing that it is part of His job to mold imperfect men into vessels fit for use. Even with Judas, knowing from the beginning that he would betray Him, He never ceased to reach out towards him to the very end. He knew the Father's will and was predisposed to not only what was desirable but also what was necessary to fulfill purpose.

In a cursory survey of Jesus' ministry, it would appear that He walked around Judea and Samaria doing good things with 12 companions who were more or less along for the ride. But as we look more closely, we see that Jesus had a purpose for the apostles far beyond the fulfillment of a biblical type. They were first and foremost to become the foundation for the propagation of Jesus' ministry beyond His death. This three and a half-year period was training and preparation so that they could be about their Father's business. Jesus trained them in many ways and set them in order to foster His ministry. Just as the tribes of Israel were ordered according their function, so Jesus set the apostles in order to serve His ministry.

Jesus broke their function in His ministry down into three areas corresponding to the three dimensions of service. He grouped the apostles into three groups of four as indicated by the four listings of the apostles in Scripture. The names of each apostle, though in different order, always fall within their particular group. Heading each group of four and always in the same positions are: position number one—Peter; position number five—Phillip; and position number nine—James, the son of Alphaeus. Judas as the betrayer is always listed last in each account.

The first group of Peter, James, John, and Andrew is separated from the other two by their closeness to Jesus. The first three of these disciples form what is called by some, Jesus' inner circle. These seem to have the highest connection in the Spirit. The second group, headed by Phillip, seems to be a liaison between the people and Jesus, while the third group seems to minister to the material needs of Jesus and His entourage.

Whatever significance we may want to assign to each group or each apostle, it does seem evident that Jesus ordered His followers according to the need of His ministry. Not all the apostles performed the same function or were privy to all the same events of Jesus' ministry. They all varied in glory one from another.

While considering this information about the order of Jesus' ministry and His disciples, we must determine proper qualification of our own ministries. Every ministry is qualified by its development in four areas. First, is the area of leadership requiring vision, integrity, and direction. Jesus filled this position in His ministry.

Second, it is qualified by its message—doctrine and purpose. Why does God call this ministry? Like Peter and those of the first group, every ministry needs those who can see the transfiguration of the third dimension. It needs those who seek to understand the coming temple, those who are of a nature that they can participate in the glory of God, and those who will not run from the agony of a garden.

Third, it is qualified by its organization. Every ministry must be organized to address the needs of those it ministers to and to handle the issues of ministry in an ordered way. This group of Jesus' apostles was uniquely qualified. Matthew gave a written account of Jesus' ministry with the preciseness of a tax collector ledgering his accounts. Nathaniel was not afraid to ask if the ministry of Jesus could amount to any good. Thomas thought seeing was believing, and Phillip, who led this group, acted as an intermediary between the general public and Jesus.

Finally, a ministry is qualified by its provision in the material world. Every ministry needs money and materials to supply the needs of the natural world. Much less is written about the duties of this group because dimensionally it is the lowest. This is not to say that Jesus valued the worth of any of the apostles greater than the others. It was their nature and preparation and His purpose that decided their position in His ministry.

What Can We Learn From the Organization of Jesus' Ministry?

If we understand His was an ordered ministry, then perhaps we can gain some helpful insight in operating ours? Perhaps we will see how to break our ministries down according to required function. Maybe we will understand in a more enlightened way those the Lord is bringing to us. We must see the need to properly raise ministry sons and establish generational order.

A seed shall serve Him; it shall be accounted to the Lord for a generation (Psalm 22:30).

Hopefully, we will see that Jesus was not just living for Himself or for His present position, but for future generations. We should come to understand that His ministry was entrusted into the hands of a few individuals; and it was their training, maturity, and success in the Spirit that would decide whether the entrustment given Him of the Father would be completed. Wise men of God know their ministry is not about themselves but about future generations. They see themselves not as the ministry, but as the part of a greater ministry leading to the coming of God's Kingdom.

Chapter Nine

———•••••———

MINISTRY OF THE SAINTS

I beseech you, brethren, (ye know the house of Stephanas, that it is the firstfruits of Achaia, and that they have addicted themselves to the ministry of the saints) (1 Corinthians 16:15).

There is a ministry to the Body; there is also a ministry of the Body. The ascension gift ministries are primarily ministry to the Body. The ministry of saints is primarily the ministry of the Body. The various types of ministry and their purpose and order in the Church are important to recognize so that we can understand how the various parts of the Body relate and how they minister to each other.

These all help bring the Church into its fullness and its ultimate purpose—the ministry of the Church to the world. The ministry of the saints is the ministry of the Body of Christ to the world. A multiplicity of ministry is not only required for the perfection of the Body but for its proper ministry to the world.

For the perfecting of the saints, for the work of the ministry, for the edifying of the body of Christ (Ephesians 4:12).

The saints were not given to the fivefold ministry for the benefit of the ministry, but the fivefold ministry is of the saints and was given to the Church for the benefit of the Body and for the equipping of the saints and for the ministry of the saints. The Church should be like a school training the saints up into a powerful army of God. Local church ministry is to minister to the saints so that the saints (which includes everyone in the Church including the ministry), can minister to the world. The Body of Christ ministering to the world in every area of occupation and influence is the ministry of the saints.

The Power of Anointing
Is the Power of Alignment

Behold, how good and how pleasant it is for brethren to dwell together in unity! It is like the precious ointment upon the head, that ran down upon the beard, even Aaron's beard: that went down to the skirts of his garments; as the dew of Hermon, and as the dew that descended upon the mountains of Zion: for there the Lord commanded the blessing, even life for evermore (Psalm 133:1-3).

Anointing always flows down and is never to touch flesh. It first touches the head (those in rule) and then the rest of the Body. A church operating in the multiplicity of ministry allows for the full anointing of God to each part. But because saints are taught to seek gifting rather than alignment, they miss the multiplying and intensifying flow of anointing.

A church whose members seek their own agendas or the personal agendas of the ministry, will never establish relationship and at best operate only in single flows of anointing. *"Thou anointest my head with oil; my cup runneth over"* (Ps. 23:5b). Saints are usually never taught that the easiest way to walk in double portions of anointing is to anoint their head (those God has placed in rule over them). If we anoint our head by coming into order and submission, then our vessel (cup) will run over.

For all seek their own, not the things which are Jesus Christ's (Philippians 2:21).

Saints who are not connected will always find a way to walk away from a local church. Many churches resort to threats or fear to keep saints, never realizing the power of relationship. Loving saints seek relationship; prideful saints and ministry seek only self. If people are bound in true relationship, trying to separate them from the Church is like trying to separate your hand from your body.

Why are some saints willing to separate from the Body for almost any reason? It is because their pride seeks self over relationship with the Body. Why are some pastors forever "whipping" the saints into shape? It is because they seek a following rather than relationship. It is impossible to have a ministry of the saints within a church if they are not first seeking relationship. It is the Body edifying itself in love that pursues the ministry of the saints.

And by the hands of the apostles were many signs and wonders wrought among the people; (and they were all with one accord in Solomon's porch) (Acts 5:12).

Fulfil ye my joy, that ye be likeminded, having the same love, being of one accord, of one mind (Philippians 2:2).

When the Bible speaks of one accord, one heart, one mind, one soul, one place, and singleness of heart, it is describing proper alignment. Things that are in proper alignment are in right relationship. If the parts of a well—the pump, the pressure tank, the piping, the valves—are properly aligned, their relationship to one another will make possible the flow of water through the well to be used for the purpose intended. A person can have all the parts of the well, but if they are not connected in proper alignment, they will be of little use.

141

The ministry of the saints, like the well, is dependent upon proper alignment. The Church often lacks relationship because it lacks a multiplicity of ministry. A local church may have all the necessary members and giftings but, like the well, if it is not in alignment, it will never be able to fulfill its purpose. The Church will never be able to bring about the biblical ministry of the saints because the anointing will not be present throughout the Body in proper measure.

> *And the multitude of them that believed were of one heart and of one soul: neither said any of them that ought of the things which he possessed was his own; but they had all things common. And with great power gave the apostles witness of the resurrection of the Lord Jesus: and great grace was upon them all (Acts 4:32-33).*

The Jerusalem church of the Book of Acts had great power because of their relationship. They operated in one heart and one soul—that is to say that they operated as a single individual, one body. This allowed the great grace of God to be upon them and Jesus to be manifested to their community. The Christian Church today does not teach the power of alignment and relationship but rather the power of gifting and the power of prosperity.

The Ministry of the Saints Requires Relationship

The ultimate purpose of ministry is the fostering of relationships among the saints, to the world and with God. The ministry of the saints is a ministry that seeks to bring those in the world into relationship with the Church and with God. As His Body, at times we see dimly, and at other times, not at all. As in gospel times, we often look for a Kingdom that speaks more of earthly power, personal achievement, and material acquisition than one of relationship with the Father and godly knowledge, wisdom, and understanding.

That the God of our Lord Jesus Christ, the Father of glory, may give unto you the spirit of wisdom and revelation in the knowledge of Him: the eyes of your understanding being enlightened; that ye may know what is the hope of His calling, and what the riches of the glory of His inheritance in the saints, and what is the exceeding greatness of His power to us-ward who believe, according to the working of His mighty power (Ephesians 1:17-19, emphasis added).

And Jesus answered him, The first of all the commandments is, Hear, O Israel; The Lord our God is one Lord: and thou shalt love the Lord thy God with all thy heart, and with all thy soul, and with all thy mind, and with all thy strength: this is the first commandment. And the second is like, namely this, Thou shalt love thy neighbour as thyself. There is none other commandment greater than these (Mark 12:29-31).

We need the spiritual enlightenment that can come only through a love relationship with the Father and with each other. The fulfillment of the Old Testament is found in these two commandments. We will never receive or walk in this love without seeking relationship. There is no greater commandment of God than for us to seek relationship by love.

Measuring Relationship

The Kingdom of God is manifested in three levels or measures of relationship. The Kingdom cannot be overcome but is itself a mechanism that brings forth change and order. Like leaven, it rises to saturate all spiritual manna (spiritual bread or the Word by which we live). As Kingdom consciousness rises in our minds, it influences and becomes part of every thought. It is hidden from the natural eye but will take dominion in every level of our spiritual relationship.

Abraham was seeking this full measure of relationship in all levels, when he instructed Sarah to take three measures of meal and make cakes (bread) in response to the visitation of the Lord in the plains of Mamre. Likewise, the apostle Paul speaks of a measure in the fullness of Christ to which we are to attain.

One becomes increasingly aware of the fact that our ability to find relationship is in large part dependent upon our ability to see and respond to the Jesus in others.

> *Give, and it shall be given unto you; good measure, pressed down, and shaken together, and running over, shall men give into your bosom. For with the same **measure** that ye mete withal it shall be measured to you again* (Luke 6:38, emphasis added).

There is a longing on the part of most to experience the supernatural, to see tangible manifestations of heavenly power via great miracles and demonstrations of spiritual power. These desires were likewise present in the masses who followed after Jesus. In large part, they followed Him to receive bread, to see miracles, and to witness a demonstration of God's power. Jesus warned of an evil and adulterous generation who sought after signs. All true signs point us to greater relationship with and love for Jesus.

Sign-seeking will never produce relationship because it is the result of people desiring the gift rather than the Giver. There is an adulterous generation—a generation who is willing to enter relationships amiss and change loyalties for personal benefit. There is also a generation being birthed who seeks the Father, not out of personal benefit, but out of desire for order, obedience, and relationship.

When Jesus walked on the earth, most did not see anything more than a man possessing tremendous power. Some attributed this power to God and others to the devil, yet most saw only a man—a gifted and unique man to be sure, but yet just a man. Jesus' purpose was to reveal the Father to mankind. To those with eyes to see, it becomes glaringly apparent why father/son order is the key to relationship in ministry.

Then said they unto Him, Where is Thy Father? Jesus answered, Ye neither know Me, nor My Father: if ye had known Me, ye should have known My Father also (John 8:19).

The Kingdom was hidden within Jesus. Only those who could see beyond the man, beyond the miracles, and beyond their own prejudices, could see into the Kingdom. These were people who desired relationship. We likewise need to learn to experience the Kingdom resident within the members of the Body of Christ—to go beyond our fears and our flesh and our preconceived ideas and see the treasure that is hidden within each saint.

Neither shall they say, Lo here! or, lo there! for, behold, the kingdom of God is within you (Luke 17:21).

A unique part of God is hid in the soul of each member, to be revealed by those wise enough to dig it out. The Kingdom is within the Body! We are not going to find relationship by seeking after miracles, or by pursuing gifted Christian ministries and personalities, or by searching the stars for Heaven's location. If the Church is to find genuine relationship, it must begin to see and fellowship with the "Jesus" within the Body. This brings new understanding to the following Scripture:

For where two or three are gathered together in My name, there am I in the midst of them (Matthew 18:20).

One final thought related to the measure of relationship: The Word *measure* is used prominently in four biblical instances, listing the dimensions of Moses' tabernacle, Solomon's temple, Ezekiel's vision of the temple, and in the apostle John's revelation of the New Jerusalem and its temple. If we looked at references to the measurement of biblical temples for their spiritual rather than their literal dimensions, perhaps we would obtain greater understanding and revelation.

The words *dimension* and *measure*, of necessity, require us to consider the object being measured in relation to its length, width, depth, and height. These measurements are spiritual, as well as literal in nature. As the apostle Paul illustrates in Ephesians chapter 3: *"That ye, being rooted and grounded in love, may be able to comprehend with all saints what is the breadth, and length, and depth, and height"* (Eph. 3:17b-18). These are not only natural measurements, but more significantly spiritual measurements of the glory of the Father and the family of God.

In another biblical reference, the word *measure* is used in this spiritual sense, such as, the measure of the fathers, the measure of faith, the measure of the gift, and the measure of rule. The point is that we don't measure relationships by a ruler of inches or yards or meters but with a spiritual measure.

Using the above as a pattern, we can see the foolishness of measuring the value or effectiveness of ministries, saints, and churches using natural, rather than spiritual, measurements. Instead of placing value on numbers, size, financial resources, ministerial prestige, and notoriety, which are natural measurements, perhaps the Spirit measures effectiveness and value in ways that we seldom consider. Perhaps the Lord judges ministries more on the investment put into saints than on resources put into promotions and buildings.

Could it be that the Father judges saints more for their faith in God than for their faith *for* things? Maybe doing the *work of God* is far more substantial in the Spirit's eyes than doing a *work for God*. Is it possible that when the Lord judges a ministry, the godliness in the saints is infinitely of more importance than the number of people in the church?

How the Work of God Is Accomplished Through a Multiplicity

God has a mission and an overwhelming mandate and wills to restore mankind to Himself. This will for man is sometimes called the "great commission" and is recorded in Mathew 28:18-20, and in various forms in the other Gospels as well. How does God accomplish this commission?

Does He send angels to do the work in place of man? No. Does He establish 2,830 denominations each competing for preeminence in the plan of God? No. Does He raise up a super-powerful individual who exceeds even the revelation and stature of the apostle Paul to lead the masses into the Kingdom? No. What He does, is send the Spirit, not into denominational structures, but into His many-membered Body who will minister to the world (the ministry of the saints).

How does His Body accomplish this commission? The members of the Body learn to align themselves in perfect relationship so that the Holy Spirit can have full control and do all His will. What brings the Body into alignment? God gives to it ministry. First, God breaks down the commission into smaller portions called ministry vision (not to be confused with dreams and visions). No one individual has the entire vision of God for the earth. He gives these ministry visions to individuals whom He sets in a certain place for a specific purpose (set ministry).

The set minister establishes the local work or church. God gathers around the set ministry those who are connected by the Spirit to the vision. These people are ordered by the set ministry according to a multiplicity of ministry and by the ministry of the saints. This is how they find their ministry in the Body. How they minister is dependent on their gifting. Their gifting is not their ministry but how the grace of God works through them to perform their ministry.

The anointing of God flows down through the alignment of the set ministry, through the multiplicity of ministry, and to the ministry of the saints. Anointing becomes the empowerment of the gifting in ministry. The Spirit thus has complete authority, and only God gets the glory for the wonder of the things done. This empowerment is controlled by His love. Flesh can't steal His glory, usurp His anointing, or disguise His love.

The will of God is stated as His commission (with mission or assignment) to His people. This mission or assignment is to restore mankind to God. Vision then becomes our portion of the assignment. Ministry is the vehicle for carrying out the vision. Gifting is how the grace of God operates through us to do our ministry. Anointing is the power of God in our gifting, and love is the motivation and force that ties these elements together, fostering relationship in the Body and with God.

> *But speaking the truth in love, may grow up into Him in all things, which is the head, even Christ: from whom the whole body fitly joined together and compacted by that which every joint supplieth, according to the effectual working in the measure of every part, maketh increase of the body unto the edifying of itself in love* (Ephesians 4:15-16).

> *Hereby perceive we the love of God, because He laid down His life for us: and we ought to lay down our lives for the brethren* (1 John 3:16).

The great force in the universe is love. Jesus gave His body for us so that we could become His Body. We lay down our lives (our personal agendas, selfish pursuits, our desire to live independent of the Body) so that we can be joined and perfected with the brethren in the Body of Christ.

148

Nor height, nor depth, nor any other creature, shall be able to separate us from the love of God, which is in Christ Jesus our Lord (Romans 8:39).

The love of God is found in Jesus, and Jesus is found or manifested in His Body if it is ordered after a multiplicity of ministry. Then the ministry of the saints can reach the world. The ministry of the saints has not yet been realized in the Church. We have been unsuccessfully trying to win the world with the fivefold ministry, but it was never their assignment. Their job was to equip and perfect the saints so that the saints could reach the world.

And He said unto them, Go ye into all the world, and preach the gospel to every creature (Mark 16:15).

The saints cannot reach the world by bringing the world into the Church, but by going out into all the world and becoming light and salt. The traditional view was and still is that God will win the world through gifted preachers who grow local churches and expand the influence of those ministries. Perhaps God's plan involves sending saints into the entire world and affecting the world in every area of commerce and social interaction. It is a plan that involves taking the Church into the world rather than bringing the world into Church.

Chapter Ten

BRINGING THE CHURCH
TO THE WORLD

But Jesus called them to Him, and saith unto them, Ye know that they which are accounted to rule over the Gentiles exercise lordship over them; and their great ones exercise authority upon them. But so shall it not be among you: but whosoever will be great among you, shall be your minister: and whosoever of you will be the chiefest, shall be servant of all. For even the Son of man came not to be ministered unto, but to minister, and to give His life a ransom for many (Mark 10:42-45).

There are three questions that can help bring the Church into the Kingdom. What does God want? What if we stopped doing everything God never told us to do? What if we changed the direction of ministry away from church projects, the advancement of the pastorate and its agenda and moved it toward establishing a ministry of saints? These questions will cause ministry to think "outside the box." If we would think outside the box, we might see the greatest time and effort of ministry should be given to building the saints. They, not our ministries, are the end of God's purpose.

Within religion there has been a misconception birthed by tradition. This is a misconception about what it means to be a minister and what it means to be a saint. The greatest calling within the Church is not to be a pastor or an apostle, but to be a saint.

All in the five-faceted ministry are first and foremost saints, and their purpose must be centered on the will of God for His saints. All saints are to become ministers—not necessarily fivefold ministers, but ministers of righteousness to the world. Unfortunately, in most places, the focus is on establishing great ministries and not maturing great saints. In the Christian world, the expression of the relationship between what is called "the ministry" and those who are thought of as saints is backward.

God did not call ministry to be kings. Our focus must not be on becoming great ministries, but on perfecting the saints. It is all too common for the local church to be built on the feudal system. The pastor is like the king or noble who provides a castle for safety and social interchange. The saints are the serfs who bring a portion of their produce to the noble in exchange for his protection and nurturing.

In most places, we have not built a church, but a feudal hierarchy. This is reminiscent of the doctrine of the Nicolaitanes, which is the separation of God's people by elevation of the clergy or laity over the other. The apostle John uses strong language to describe this thing God hates, for it hinders the manifestation of the true Church of God. *"But this thou hast, that thou hatest the deeds of the Nicolaitanes, which I also hate"* (Rev. 2:6).

Jesus said the rulers of the Gentiles lord over them, and the great ones exercise authority upon them. Ministry should not lord—that is, exercise rule as a divinity or nobleman, nor should they exercise authority upon the saints. This does not mean that they do not exercise authority, but they do not exercise authority upon the saints, meaning as a taskmaster or supreme being. The following verse is Jesus' admonishment to His followers who desire greatness.

But it shall not be so among you: but whosoever will be great among you, let him be your minister; and whosoever will be chief among you, let him be your servant (Matthew 20:26).

Ministry can be properly provided only from a position of a servant and never as lord. Being our example, Jesus states that even He did not come to be ministered to, but to minister and to give His life a ransom. A ransom is a price paid to redeem something lost or stolen. Are we as ministry willing to pay the price of becoming true servants so that we may become vessels from which can be ministered the grace, mercy, and love of God? Are we willing to be a ransom rather than a king?

Too often, the Church is like a major league sporting franchise; the ministry is the team and the saints are the spectators. They fill the seats of the arena to view the spiritual exploits of their favorite ministry. The saints, for the most part, do not minister but watch. Their purpose is to provide faithfulness and financial support so that the ministry can indulge in its favorite activities and, in the process, fascinate and delight the saints.

The saints are spectators. They are not allowed to participate but only observe. In exchange for their monetary payment and faithful attendance, the saints are given relief from the normal pressures of life and made to feel part of the team. The above, of course, is an oversimplification, but it does illustrate the disorder in a church that does not allow for a multiplicity of ministry and which fails to recognize the ultimate purpose of any church, which is the effectual operation of the ministry of the saints.

And He gave some, apostles; and some, prophets; and some, evangelists; and some, pastors and teachers; for the perfecting of the saints, for the work of the ministry, for the edifying of the body of Christ: till we all come in the unity of the faith, and of the knowledge of the Son of God, unto a perfect man, unto the measure of the stature of the fulness of Christ: that we henceforth be no more children, tossed to and fro, and carried about with every wind of doctrine, by the sleight of men, and cunning craftiness, whereby they lie in wait to deceive; but speaking the truth in love, may grow up into Him in all things, which is the head, even Christ: from whom the whole body fitly joined together and compacted by that which every joint supplieth, according to the effectual working in the measure of every part, maketh increase of the body unto the edifying of itself in love (Ephesians 4:11-16).

The purpose of everyone in the five-faceted ministry falls into three primary areas. All church ministry is to do the following: perfect the saints, provide for the work of their ministry, and edify the Body of Christ. It is all about the saints! It is about perfecting the saints, meaning that ministry must bring saints into maturity and wholeness. It is about the work of the ministry, literally their ministry by equipping, instructing, and confirming saints into their gifting, purpose, calling, and destiny. It is about edification of the Body by allowing for the rule of the Holy Spirit and the proper connection of the Body and the ministry of that Body to the world. Unless the fivefold or five-faceted ministry is directed toward the saints, it cannot fulfill its purpose.

Church is not the end of God's intention, but the vehicle that is able to bring forth His Kingdom. The local church is a school for aligning, confirming, and training the saints of God. The restoration of the world back into order with God has never rested upon the shoulders of the ministry, but upon the saints. The local church's ultimate responsibility is to mature the saints of God so they can reach the world and establish His Kingdom. Ministry ought to be teachers and instructors in the King's house to raise His children into maturity.

"Till we all come in the unity of the faith, and of the knowledge of the Son of God, unto a perfect man" (Eph. 4:13). The purpose of ministry within the local church is to make out of the many, one Body. We need the fivefold ministry until we (plural) all become a (singular) perfect man.

This is why church must become a school to mature and then release saints into their ministry. *"I will build My church; and the gates of hell shall not prevail against it"* (Mt. 16:18b). The gates of hell, which are defensive devices to keep people bound from escaping, cannot hold back the Church because the Church has been given keys to unlock the gates that have kept so many imprisoned.

> *Now I say, That the heir, as long as he is a child, differeth nothing from a servant, though he be lord of all; but is under tutors and governors until the time appointed of the father. Even so we, when we were children, were in bondage under the elements of the world: but when the fulness of the time was come, God sent forth His Son, made of a woman, made under the law, to redeem them that were under the law, that we might receive the adoption of sons. And because ye are sons, God hath sent forth the Spirit of His Son into your hearts, crying, Abba, Father. Wherefore thou art no more a servant, but a son; and if a son, then an heir of God through Christ* (Galatians 4:1-7).

The children of the King are put under tutors and governors until the time of their manifestation as sons. These are the three dimensions of our spiritual progression and speak of the need for preparation among all saints: Tutors are instructors or trainers who impart knowledge and establish discipline; governors provide oversight, administration, and direction; mature son-ship allows the Christian to "graduate" from being under tutors and governors and participating in the right of all sons, to the inheritance found in the ministry of the saints. There are certain principals of ministry necessary in order for the three "acts of the Kingdom" to come forth.

First: Those in a position of authority over God's people must not work to become "great ministers" or "great ministries."

This is a gross misunderstanding of what it means to minister. If ministry exalts itself by seeking its own fame, position, and agenda, it humbles God and His Kingdom. We should kneel before God, not He before our plans and the work of our hands.

Second: God did not call the fivefold ministry to become kings but servants.

Only a servant mentality will manifest a Kingdom ministry. We need to learn what it means to be a servant. Ministry that makes the saints serfs and ministers royalty is not proper ministry.

Third: The purpose of the fivefold ministry is to put the saints into their ministry.

What is commonly called ministry has no real ministry if it does not bring forth the ministry of the saints. Using the saints to provide a platform, position, and support structure for our "ministry" negates ministry's true purpose and hinders saints from ever finding theirs.

Fourth: The position of ministry is to be teachers and instructors in the King's house.

We are to raise His children to maturity. We all must see ourselves as saints. Our position as saint is greater than any position we may have in the fivefold ministry. True saints are ones who are fathered. True fivefold ministry will provide training leading to maturity and take the people of God from being under tutors and governors into fatherhood.

Out of Zion, the perfection of beauty, God hath shined
(Psalm 50:2).

Zion is the perfection of God's beauty. The saints of God
who become His spiritual house show forth the glory of God.
"The riches of the glory of His inheritance in the saints" (Eph.
1:18b), speaks not of our inheritance but of the inheritance of
Jesus. We are the inheritance of Jesus. There are three glories;
the glory of the sun, moon, and stars is the glory of God in
three dimensions.

> *But God giveth it a body as it hath pleased Him, and to*
> *every seed his own body. All flesh is not the same flesh:*
> *but there is one kind of flesh of men, another flesh of*
> *beasts, another of fishes, and another of birds. There are*
> *also celestial bodies, and bodies terrestrial: but the glory of*
> *the celestial is one, and the glory of the terrestrial is*
> *another. There is one glory of the sun, and another glory of*
> *the moon, and another glory of the stars: for one star dif-*
> *fereth from another star in glory. So also is the resurrec-*
> *tion of the dead* (1 Corinthians 15:38-42a).

Saints need to know who they are. They are the sons of
God. God created a son of God in Adam to have relationship
with Him. Later, this relationship was broken through sin, so
the Son of God, Jesus, was sent to redeem that which was lost
by His son, Adam. In the end of time, God is sending another
son, the many-membered Body of Christ to bring forth the
Kingdom. We are the sons of God! When saints truly grasp
who they are, they will turn the world upside down—the world
upside down is the Kingdom.

The glory of God comes in three dimensions. It first
shines as the sun. The glory of the sun is the glory of salvation.
Salvation brings with it great light. It separates us from darkness and illuminates our path.

157

The glory of the moon is the glory of the soul. The soul like the moon is a reflection of the sun. The moon has no light of its own. A soul that is redeemed will be a reflection of the Son of God.

The glory of the stars is the glory of the saints. It is the highest glory, for it manifests the glory of God in all the universe. The saints ruled by Jesus will bring restoration of the *uni*-verse—*uni* meaning one and verse meaning song or word. The ministry of the saints will restore the creation back to the one song and one word of God.

> *Therefore sprang there even of one, and him as good as dead, so many as the stars of the sky in multitude, and as the sand which is by the sea shore innumerable* (Hebrews 11:12).

> *And they that be wise shall shine as the brightness of the firmament; and they that turn many to righteousness as the stars for ever and ever* (Daniel 12:3).

The presence of God within His saints shall shine as stars and turn many to righteousness. We shall become the habitation of the Almighty. This is our destiny. A multiplicity of ministry provides the order to bring forth the Kingdom and fulfill our destiny. As ministry reorders itself according to the biblical pattern, the manifestation of the ever-present Kingdom of God will grow in its influence and reality. The sound of the seventh angel of great heavenly voices will be heard in the earth saying, *"The kingdoms of this world are become the kingdoms of our Lord, and of His Christ; and He shall reign for ever and ever"* (Rev. 11:15b).

GLOSSARY
OF
MINISTRY TERMS

In the Church world, there are multiple definitions for every biblical term. To equip the reader with ministry terms as defined in this writing, we have provided the ensuing glossary. The following is an explanation of the list of terms used in this book to describe ministry terms.

Fivefold Ministry

From Ephesians chapter 4. Sometimes referred to as "ascension gift ministries" because when Jesus *"ascended on high, He led captivity captive, and gave gifts unto men."* The gifts He gave are described as the apostle, prophet, evangelist, pastor, and teacher. Some combine the last two into a single office. The hand in the Bible designates a type of ministry. The *fivefold ministry* is like the fingers on a hand. They are described as follows.

Apostle

The *apostle* governs. He is like the thumb that works in conjunction with the other fingers to perform tasks. As the thumb governs the hand, so the apostle has been set in the Church to establish government. He is sent forth by the Spirit and has the ministry of establishment.

Prophet

The *prophet* guides. He is like the index finger pointing the way. The prophet has the ministry from Jeremiah chapter 1—to build and plant. In order to do this, he is often called on to root out, pull down, destroy, and throw down the things man has built through the work of his own hands. The prophet speaks to the people for God.

Evangelist

The *evangelist* gathers. He is like the middle finger, which has the farthest reach. The evangelist reaches out into the world to gather in. He also reaches out into the Church to evangelize the saints. The words *evangelist* and *preach* come from the same Greek root. An evangelist is a preacher of the gospel as opposed to a teacher. He speaks by the Spirit to elicit a response from the heart.

Pastor

The *pastor* guards. He is like the ring finger—the covenant finger. The Greek word for *pastor* is the same as the word for *shepherd*. A shepherd cares for the flock—the sheep of God. The pastor provides nurturing, care, and protection.

Teacher

The *teacher* grounds. He is like the pinky finger. When the hand is made into a fist to pound or ground something, it is this finger that makes contact. The teacher matures the saints by establishing them in the Word. The Greek word for *teacher* is derived from the same word as *doctrine*. The teacher establishes saints in doctrine. He speaks by the Spirit to evoke a response from the mind.

Set Ministry

Set ministry is the one who is set over a work by God. Unlike religious systems, God establishes any work (including a local church) by giving a vision to a man and commissioning that man to establish the work. The set minister may be gifted in any of the fivefold ministry gifts, but the office of a set minister is the office of an apostle. God always chooses a man, never a system. Those who aid the set minister in the establishment of a work can also be viewed as part of the set ministry, as Timothy was to Paul or as in Acts 14:23. Set ministry is one of the three categories of church government in the New Testament. See also: Numbers 27:16-18; Ezekiel 33:7; Luke 7:8; Acts 15:16; 1 Corinthians 4:9; 11:34; 12:18,28; Titus 1:5.

Bishop

A *bishop* is an overseer with the responsibility of leadership over a church. The words *bishop* and *elder* are often used interchangeably in the Bible; see Acts 20:17,28; Titus 1:5,7. By biblical hypothesis and historical reference, a bishop can be viewed as a type of elder. The distinction could be made that a bishop is an elder with oversight over other ministries or more than one work.

Elder

Elders were those given oversight of the nation of Israel and, in the New Testament, of the Church. Elders were ordained by set ministry in every church to provide oversight; see Titus 1:5; Acts 14:23. The office of elder is one of the three categories of church government. There were various types of elders in the Church with specific duties; see First Timothy 5:17. They have power in the lives of saints; see James 5:14-15. The elder's position required special protection for the good of the Church; see First Timothy 5:19. They were given authority to restore those who opposed the truth; see Titus 1:9. They required a high standard for qualification; see Titus 1:6-9. There are elders of the local church, and there are also elders of the Church at large; see First Peter 5:1 and Second John 1.

Presbytery

A *presbytery* is an assembly of elders in the Church; see First Timothy 4:14. The Greek word, *presbuterion,* is also used of the Sanhedrin in Luke. A presbytery as used herein refers to a "pastors' council." These are elders of the Church at large who are gathered around a set minister to advise and support.

Deacon

A *deacon* is a servant of the church. The Greek word, *diakonos,* from which the word *deacon* is derived, is translated

30 times as "servant." A high standard of character is required for a deacon; see First Timothy 3:8-13. This office of servant-hood allows for the greater order and care of the Church; see Acts 6:1-6. The office of deacon is one of the three categories of church government.

Body of Christ

The *Body of Christ* is often thought of as all saints, collectively, who are alive today; see First Corinthians 12:27. The Body of Christ, as used herein, is the connection of all the members of Christ. It is the proper connection of these members that allow Christ to become visible to the world. The return of Jesus is first manifesting in His coming and appearing in His Body. Multiplicity of ministry is the proper ministry order of this Body to itself and the world.

Church Government

Government is the administration and rule of the Church by the Holy Spirit. God has established certain ministry offices to facilitate that rule. If ministry is properly aligned, then the Holy Spirit will have dominion over the Church. If not, then the governance of the Church will be largely of men and not of God. All Church government fits into one of three categories: gifts, administrations, operations; see First Corinthians 12:4-6. These correspond to the New Testament offices of set ministry, elders, and deacons and have their type in the Old Testament priesthood as well. Jesus likewise followed Old Testament type of the government of Israel. Jesus established three categories: apostles (the ministry of establishment); the 70 (elders)—see Luke 10:1,17, Numbers 11:25; and the disciples (deacons).

Church Council

The *Church council* is a body of elders or leadership. It is the presbytery giving direction to the local church and the

Church at large. These church councils of elders gave oversight to the local church and the Church as a whole. This is the group that was to make the judgments such as the ones spoken of by Paul in First Corinthians 6, and made decisions in Antioch (see Acts 15:2). Barnabas and Paul were sent by the council in Antioch to the council in Jerusalem. In Acts 15, it is the council or presbytery of Jerusalem that hears the issue of circumcision, in part, because those who caused the contention came from there and were under the authority of the Jerusalem church. Even in this case, brought before the council, it was through a single individual, James, whom the Spirit brought forth the ruling which the council agreed *"for it seemed good to the Holy Ghost, and to us"* Acts 15:28b. Note: Biblical councils are not board decisions ("Four in favor, three against, the ayes have it"), but confirmations of the voice of the Spirit. The council at Jerusalem sent their report back to Antioch. This is how proper Church government should work between local churches.

Ministry of the Saints

Ministry of the saints is the ministry of the Body to itself and especially to the world; see Hebrews 6:10; Ephesians 4:16. *Ministry of the saints* is the ministry of the Church to the world as opposed to religious approaches where "soul winning" methods and the clergy work toward reaching the lost. The Church is to school the saints, and the fivefold ministry are the instructors of the spiritual school for edification, equipping, and to aid the saints in their ministries; see Ephesians 4:11-12. The entire Body has been called to minister to the world; see First Corinthians 16:15.

Ministry Sons

The order of ministry, as well as the Kingdom, is the order of *father and son.* A set minister may be a ministry father to the entire congregation (as Abraham is a father of us all), but God brings specific individuals in connection with us in ministry. We refer to those who are truly connected to a minister in the same way as Elisha was to Elijah, Peter was to Jesus, or Titus was to Paul—*as ministry sons.*

Multiplicity of Ministry

Multiplicity means many-faceted ministry. Ministry in the Church is not just a single individual or office. The Body is made up of multiple members, each having a ministry. The ministry of these multiple members and the offices given them form the multiplicity of ministry. When ministry comes only through a single individual or a few individuals, the fullness of the ministry of the Holy Spirit is not in operation in the Church. This creates a weak and immature Church and not the manifestation of the full Christ to and through the Body.

The fivefold ministry, and others, are a gift to the Church.

Ministry Gift

A distinction must be made between gifting and ministry. *Ministry gifts* are doma gifts that involve the measure of rule as opposed to charisma gifts, which are gifts given to every believer by the Spirit.

Spiritual Gifts

Many have wrongly assumed that their gifting is their ministry. Gifting is not ministry, but the empowerment and mechanism God gives us to accomplish our ministry. God's grace in ministry works through our gifts; see Romans 12:6 and First Corinthians 3:10. When someone declares their gifting to be their ministry, he or she usually lacks understanding about their identity. In exalting the gift, they fail to find their true purpose. There are many gifts among them—helps, ministry, tongues, healing, prophecy, administration, encouragement, salvation, etc. The empowerment of God's grace in any area of our life is a gift. Ministry is how we are called to serve God; gifts are how we are empowered by God to minister.

CONTACT INFORMATION

MAILING ADDRESS:

Mark Hanby Ministries
P.O. Box 8093
Chattanooga, TN 37414

PHONE:

(423) 510-8383

FAX:

(423) 510-8765

TO ORDER RESOURCES:

Toll-Free 1-800-649-3420

WEB ADDRESS:

www.hanby.org

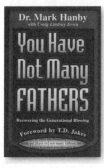
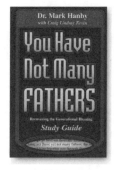

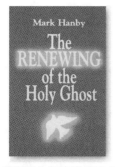
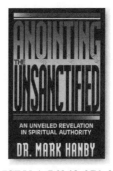

Additional copies of this book and other
book titles from DESTINY IMAGE are
available at your local bookstore.

For a bookstore near you, call 1-800-722-6774.

Send a request for a catalog to:

Destiny Image® Publishers, Inc.

P.O. Box 310
Shippensburg, PA 17257-0310

*"Speaking to the Purposes of God for This
Generation and for the Generations to Come"*

For a complete list of our titles,
visit us at www.destinyimage.com